WAR-TIME PROSECUTIONS AND MOB VIOLENCE

Involving the rights of free speech, free press and peaceful assemblage.

[*From April 1, 1917 to March 1, 1919*]

This list of cases is compiled from the correspondence and press clippings of the National Civil Liberties Bureau. It is by no means a complete record. The Bureau would appreciate information about other cases.

**Fredonia Books
Amsterdam, The Netherlands**

War-Time Prosecutions and Mob Violence:
Involving the Rights of Free Speech, Free Press
and Peaceful Assemblage

by
National Civil Liberties Bureau

ISBN: 1-4101-0445-1

Copyright © 2004 by Fredonia Books

Reprinted from the 1919 edition

Fredonia Books
Amsterdam, The Netherlands
http://www.fredoniabooks.com

All rights reserved, including the right to reproduce this book, or portions thereof, in any form.

In order to make original editions of historical works available to scholars at an economical price, this facsimile of the original edition of 1919 is reproduced from the best available copy and has been digitally enhanced to improve legibility, but the text remains unaltered to retain historical authenticity.

War-Time Prosecutions and Mob Violence

AN ANNOTATED LIST OF CASES

THIS briefly annotated list of prosecutions under war statutes and cases of mob violence due to the war is published as a matter of record for those interested. The list does not include cases of enemy aliens (except one of mob violence), spies or violations of the draft act by men of military age, except a few cases under the September 12, 1918, registration and the cases carried to the United States Supreme Court to test the constitutionality of the law. Further information about the more important cases will be furnished by the Bureau on request.

The cases are set forth under the following classifications:

I. Mob Violence — 164
   1. For alleged personal disloyalty — 123
      a. General Cases — 101
      b. Forced by mobs to kiss the flag (a special group of cases so classified because of their number) — 22
   2. Industrial causes: involving primarily the I. W. W. — 18
   3. Political causes: involving primarily the Non-Partisan League — 23

II. Criminal Prosecutions.
   1. Espionage Act and Treason Cases.
      a. Convictions — 158
          (1) For statements in private conversation or correspondence — 102
          (2) For statements in public address or public print — 39
          (3) For distributing literature — 17
      b. Cases pending March 1, 1919 — 30
      c. Acquittals — 34
   2. Obstructing the Draft Act — 18
   3. Cases under War-time State and Local Laws — 13

    4. Prosecutions Specifically Involving I. W. W. Activity 19
       a. Conspiracies to violate various federal statute 5
       b. Convictions for criminal syndicalism and similar charges 14

III. Interference by Public Officials with the Right of Peaceful Assemblage 23
    a. General 11
    b. Non Partisan League 12

IV. Search and Seizure 45
    a. I. W. W. 10
    b. International Bible Students' Ass'n 9
    c. All others 28

V. Conscientious Objectors in Prison under Court Martial Sentence 179

VI. Miscellaneous Cases of Dismissal from the Public Service for Alleged Anti-war Views or Activities 30

    The cases are arranged in the order of their occurrence. An alphabetical index to cases is given on page 49.

    It will be noted that by far the largest proportion of all the cases throughout involve members of the I. W. W., Socialist Party and Non-Partisan League. Of those cases which do not, all but a comparative few involve citizens of German descent.

    That hundreds of cases have not come to our attention through press clippings is evident from the published statements of the Attorney General setting forth the number of prosecutions instituted and convictions obtained.

    The report of the Attorney-General for the year 1918 contains statistics of the enforcement of war-time statutes up to and including June 30th, 1918. These figures show a total of 988 prosecutions instituted: 363 cases have resulted in convictions; 57 prosecutions terminated with acquittal and 72 have been dismissed or dropped. On June 30th, 1918, there were 496 cases pending. In connection with these figures, it should be borne in mind that they represent cases and not individuals. In many cases more than one person is involved. Two prosecutions terminated since June 30th last have yielded 144 individual defendants convicted. The Department of Justice has declined to furnish us with further figures and to supply us with a list of persons indicted or convicted.

    Figures made public on June 8th, 1918, indicate that under the act making threats against the President a criminal offense, there had been a total of 60 persons prosecuted, of whom 23 pleaded guilty, 2 were dismissed, 12 convicted, and 2 acquitted. Twenty-one cases were then pending.

As compared with these figures the cases under the Espionage Act in the Bureau's list cover about 22% of the total, only a handful of the pending cases having been brought to our attention.

I. MOB VIOLENCE

Including all reported cases of violence to the person by groups of citizens acting without authority of law. It is significant that in only two cases (Robert P. Prager and the Bisbee I. W. W. Deportation) who were the mob leaders prosecutors.

1. For Alleged Personal Disloyalty.
a. General Cases.

4/8/17. **Baltimore, Md.**—Peace meeting addressed by **David Starr Jordan** attacked by mob.

——— **New York City.**—During the summer of 1917 many meeting of the Socialist Party and the Friends of Irish Freedom were broken up by soldier mobs.

7/2/17. **Boston, Mass.—Peace parade** of Socialist Party broken up and headquarters wrecked by mob of soldiers and sailors.

8/23/17. **York, S. C.—Rev. W. T. Sims,** negro preacher, lynched for alleged opposition to the draft.

9/9/17. **Milwaukee, Wis.—Several Italians** shot in street riot after a loyalty meeting.

10/2/17. **Pasadena, Cal.**—Conference of **Christian Pacifists** broken up by mob of Home Guards.

10/18/17.**New York, N. Y.**—Two meeting of Columbia students to protest against the expulsion of **Professors Cattell** and **Dana** broken up by mob of Naval Reserves.

10/30/17. **Newport, Ky.—Rev. Herbert S. Bigelow,** a prowar radical, kidnapped and horsewhipped by mob "in the name of the women and children of Belgium."

11/15/17 **Newport, Ark.—Rev. J. H. Ellis,** negro preacher, held for 96 days on flimsy charge of "treason." When released from jail beaten by mob of white citizens and officials.

11/18/17. **New York, N. Y.**—Dry goods store on upper east side wrecked by mob of Italians because proprietor was alleged not to have paid proper respect to the Italian flag.

11/22/17. **Osakis, Minn.—E. H. Stratemeyer** tarred and feathered for alleged disloyalty.

12/4/17. **Hugo, Colo.—Henry Dutsch,** tarred and feathered by Vigilantes for alleged seditious utterances.

12/10/17. **St. Louis, Mo.—Emmett Oburn** beaten for neglect to stand up while Star Spangled Banner was being played at a meeting.

12/17/17. **Clayton, N. J.—Albert M. Canter,** school teacher, driven from town by mob of citizens for alleged disloyal remarks.

12/25/17. **Brenham, Tex.—Six German farmers** whipped to make them subscribe to the Red Cross.

12/28/17. **Audobon, Ia.—Rev. W. A. Starck** and **Fred Tennegkeit** beaten and nearly hanged for alleged seditious utterances. Saved from mob by dupty sheriffs.

1/5/18. **Hartford, Conn.—Maximilian Von Hoegen** beaten, nose broken, forced to kiss flag.

1/13/18. **Philadelphia, Pa.—Paul Beilfuss,** rescued by police from mob which threatened to lynch him for disloyal remarks.

1/22/18. **Mitchell, S. D.—Wm. C. Rempfer,** deported after Socialist State Convention broken up by police.

1/28/18. **Elkins, W. Va.—L. H. Keenan,** Socialist lawyer, tarred and feathered for alleged disloyalty.

2/12/18. **Staunton, Ill.—Severino Oberden,** a labor organizer, and **J. L. Metzen,** his attorney, beaten by mob in police station at Staunton, Ill. Later tarred. Many other cases of violence in this mining region for alleged disloyalty, notably Marysville, Hillsboro, Worden, Mt. Olive, Gillespie and Williamson.

3/13/18. **Ottumwa, Ia.—Leon Battig,** a teacher, paited yellow by a mob on suspicion of disloyalty.

3/16/18. **Scotland, S. D.—Wm. Rempfer,** Socialist State Secretary, and **August Friederich** driven out of town by threat of tar and feathers.

3/21/18. **Altus, Okla.—O. F. Westbrook and Henry Hoffman** beaten, tarred and feathered for alleged disloyalty.

3/20/18. **Yerington, Nev.—Elmer White** beaten with iron cat-o'-nine tails for disloyal remarks.

3/23/18. **Christopher, Ill.—Rev. John Kovalsky** and two others tarred and feathered for alleged disloyalty.

3/25/18. **Benton, Ill.—Mrs. Frances Bergen,** a Bohemian, ridden on a rail by mob of Loyalty Leaguers for alleged pro-Germanism.

3/25/18. **Duluth, Minn.—Gust Lundin,** Socialist, tarred and feathered by Knights of Liberty.

3/28/18. **Clarksville, Ark.—Frank Oberlee,** tarred, feathered and driven out of town.

3/28/18. **Hartford, Ark.—Six alleged pro-Germans** who were later declared loyal by agents of Dept. of Justice, beaten, forced to kiss the flag and thrown into jail.

3/31/18. **Ashland, Wis.—Prof. E. A. Schimmel,** tarred and feathered by mob.

4/2/18. **Lasalle, Ill.—Dr. J. C. Bienneman** ducked in canal and ordered out of town after being forced to kiss the flag. The stores of **Henry Mueller** and **Regas Bros.** were painted yellow.

4/2/18. **Emerson, Neb.—Rudolph Schwopke** tarred and feathered for alleged refusal to contribute to Red Cross.

4/3/18. **Sioux Falls, S. D.**—Windows of the **Deutscher Herold,** edited by **Conrad Kornmann,** painted yellow by mob.

4/4/18. **Sulphur, Okla.—H. C. Capers,** 72 years old, head shaved by crowd of men awaiting draft call, for alleged pro-Germanism.

4/5/18. **Sioux Falls, S. D.**—Offices of ex-U. S. Senator **R. F. Pettigrew** painted yellow by mob.

4/5/18. **Collinsville, Ill.—Robert P. Prager,** lynched by mob because of alleged pro-German utterances. Mob leaders tried and acquitted.

4/6/18. **Jefferson City, Mo.—Fritz Monal** whipped and forced to kiss the flag.

4/7/18. **Seward, Neb.—William Grats** tarred and feathered for alleged pro-Germanism.

4/8/18. **Mounds, Ill.—Norman M. Harris,** editor, beaten by a mob for alleged disloyal utterances.

4/8/18. **Hartford, Conn.**—Home Guards broke up Socialist rally.

4/8/18. **West Salisbury, Pa. Charles Klinge** beaten, made to walk along the street with a dog chain around his neck, forced to kiss the flag and ducked for alleged disloyal remarks.

4/9/18. **Monroe, N. Y.—A. C. Richter,** beaten until unconscious for remarks opposing the draft.

4/10/18. **Elk City, Okla.—Rev. Wm. M. Hicks,** tarred and feathered for promoting World Peace League.

4/11/18. **Ashland, Wis.—Adolph Anton,** tarred and feathered for alleged pro-Germanism.

4/11/18. **Salt Lake City, Utah.—Wm. Prisse,** thrown into a dough bin and nearly smothered for alleged pro-German remarks.

4/12/18. **Omaha, Neb.—Mrs. Margaret Selby,** beaten by Lithuanian women for alleged insult to the flag.

4/12/18. **Muskogee, Okla.—James Holt** tarred and feathered for refusal to buy liberty bonds.

4/13/18. **Santa Fe, N. M.—John M. Birkner,** tarred and feathered by convicts in prison while held on charge of disloyalty.

4/13/18. **Medford, Ore.—George Maynard,** member International Bible Students' Assn., iron cross painted on body, **driven** from town. **Rev. E. P. Taliaferro** driven out.

4/13/18. **Montrose, Mich.—Mrs. Harley Stafford,** tarred and feathered for "disloyal remarks."

4/14/18. **Lincoln, Neb.**—House of **Rev. George Allenbach** painted yellow for his refusal to participate in a liberty loan rally.

4/14/18. **Holland, O.—Three men** tarred and feathered and made to kiss the flag.

4/15/18. **Kansas City, Mo.Three men** painted yellow by fellow workmen for alleged remark, "To hell with the Liberty Loan."

4/15/18. **Clovis, N. M.—T. Smith,** a Socialist, tarred and feathered for refusal to buy Liberty Bonds.

4/16/18. **Woodlawn, Pa.—Three Austrian workmen** tarred for alleged disloyalty.

4/16/18. **Tulsa, Okla.—John Kubecka,** beaten, tarred and feathered by the "Knights of Liberty" for alleged disloyal remarks.

4/17/18. **Pittsburg, Pa.—Leo J. Eschman,** mobbed by 300 munition workers, led by girls.

4/17/18. **Newellton, La.—Wm. A. Hunter,** 68 years old, tarred and feathered for not buying Liberty Bonds, though he had bought $5,000 worth.

4/19/18. **Collinsville, Okla.—Henry Rheimer,** hanged by mob till almost dead because suspected of disloyalty.

4/19/18. **Arlington, S. D.**—Buildings, trees and fence posts on the farm of **August Lieske** painted yellow for refusal to buy bonds.

4/20/18. **Berkeley, Cal.**—Tent tabernacle of the Church of the Living God burnt down by mob of men and boys because of alleged pacifist beliefs of the sect. **Rev. Josiah Sykes** and two elders ducked in the baptismal tank.

4/20/18. **El Centro, Cal.—J. E. Morgan,** announced to speak at a Mooney meeting, kidnaped and run out of town in an automobile by a so-called citizens' committee.

4/21/18. **Firewater, Ore.—Unknown person,** rescued from mob which threatened to lynch him for distributing circular attacking suppression of "The Finished Mystery."

4/22/18. **McPherson. Kan.—Walter Cooperider,** tarred and feathered for alleged seditious remarks. His father, a bed-ridden man of 90 years, forced to kiss the flag.

4/22/18. **Las Vegas, N. M.—Louis A. Lee** painted yellow by fellow employes fo rrefusal to buy Liberty Bonds.

4/22/18. **Canonsburg, Pa.—Stephen Melanos,** a Greek, thrown into a creek for refusing to buy a Liberty Bond.

4/22/18. **Pendleton, Ore.—Clifford T. Metz,** attacked by mob for distributing circulars attacking the suppression of "The Finished Mystery."

4/23/18. **Wynnewood, Okla.—Claud Watson,** a farmer, tarred and feathered by 50 drafted men waiting to entrain. Negro was hired to lash his back.

4/25/18. **Bessemer, Ala.—J. Will McNabb,** handcuffed to a post for three hours for alleged disloyalty.

4/26/18. **New Bruswick, N. J.—S. H. Chovenson,** Rutgers student, secretary Socialist local, covered with molasses and feathers by a mob of business men for refusal to buy a bond and to aid the Red Cross.

4/27/18. **Pittsburg. Pa.—Unknown foreigner,** tarred and feathered for making remarks against the Liberty Loan.

4/27/18. **San Francisco, Cal.—Carl Schultz,** intimidated by "Knights of Liberty" who placed rope around his neck and caused him to leave town.

4/27/18. **Excelsior Spring, Mo.—Otto Scharf and Rudolph Gustoff,** painted yellow and forced to kiss the flag by mob.

4/30/18. **Walnut Ridge, Ark.—Charles Franke, E. J. French, W. B. Duncan and C. B. Griffen,** taken from jail and tarred and feathered for selling "The Kingdom News," a periodical of the International Bible Students' Assn.

4/30/18. **Robinson, Pa.—Albert Phillips,** tarred and feathered by Austrians for refusal to buy bonds and support Y. M. C. A. and Red Cross.

5/2/18. **San Jose, Cal.—George Koetzer,** tarred, feathered and tied to a cannon in a public park by "Knights of Liberty" for alleged disloyal remarks.

5/2/18. **Richmond, Cal.—Guido Poenisch,** tarred and feathered by masked "Knights of Liberty" for alleged disloyalty.

5/2/18. **San Jose, Cal.—H. Steinmolz** hanged until unconscious, tied to a tree and later taken away in an auto by "Knights of Liberty" for alleged disloyalty.

5/6/18.—**Birmingham, Alabama.**—The home of **M. V. Hale** dynamited for refusal to cease activities as A. F. of L. organizer.

5/7/18. **Avoca, Pennsylvania.—Barney Walukus** strung up thirty feet from the ground and a fire hose played on him by fellow employes for refusing to buy a bond.

5/7/18. **San Rafael, Cal.—Henry Zang,** an alleged pro-German, kidnapped, his hair was clipped in the shape of a cross and he was tied to a tree in front of the courthouse.

5/8/18. **Klamath Falls, Mont.—J. W. Tyrrel** driven out of town for alleged disloyalty.

5/10/18. **Henrietta, Oklahoma—Chris Wagoner** taken from jail, painted a bright red and given 20 lashes for alleged disloyalty.

5/21/18. **Spencer, S. D.—Hart Duxbury** tarred and feathered for refusal to buy Liberty Bonds or contribute to the Red Cross.

5/23/18. **Seattle, Wash.—Joe Polaris** tarred and feathered and placed on interurban trolley clad only in a gunnysack for alleged seditious remarks.

5/23/18. **St. Paul, Minn.—Gus Tummerscheit** bound, dragged several hundred feet and tied to a telegraph pole by fellow workmen for alleged disloyal utterances.

5/25/18. **El Paso, Texas—Lubi Lara** and **Jose Villareal** tarred and feathered by fellow employes for refusal to buy Liberty Bonds.

5/27/18. **New York, N. Y.—Carl Peterson** badly beaten by mob for alleged remark that he hoped Germany would win the war.

6/10/18. **Buffalo, N. Y.—Jacob W. Oswald** painted yellow by mob of fellow workmen for alleged seditious remarks.

6/22/18. **San Francisco, Cal.—George Mattel** tarred and feathered by fellow employes for alleged refusal to buy war saving stamps.

7/6/18. **Muskogee, Okla.—James Holt,** ex-U. S. deputy marshal tarred and feathered for alleged seditious statements, refusal to buy bonds or contribute to war activities.

7/23/18. **Vicksburg, Miss.—Dave Cook** tarred and feathered for alleged disloyalty.

7/23/18. **Vicksburg, Miss.—Dr. J. C. Miller** tarred and feathered for alleged disloyalty.

7/24/18. **Vicksburg, Miss.**—Two negro women tarred and feathered because they were said to have refused to work.

7/27/18. **New York, N. Y.—Carl Netreba** beaten by mob who accused him of tearing down an American flag.

10/1/18. **Fort Wayne, Ind.**—Mob of 600 forced **Max Vonderau to raise flag in front of his house.**

10/17/18. **Appleton, Wis.** — **Dan Schultze, Wm. Bates, Charles Drenks, August Julius, H. A. Holzman, Louis Becker** and **Frank Julius** coerced into buying their "quota" of Liberty Bonds by a committee of the Council of Defense.

11/—/18. **Brawley, Cal.—James Ross** dragged behind an automobile, beaten, tarred and feathered supposedly for refusal to buy Liberty Bonds but probably because of his opposition to the vice interests of the town.

b. Mob Violence—Forced by Mobs to Kiss the Flag.

12/20/17. **Pine Bluff, Ark.—George Carlisle.**

2/2/18. **Canton, O.—Harry Rogalski.**

2/28/18. **Connellsville, Pa.—Tony Senkis,** also painted green by the mob.

2/28/18. Trenton, N. J.—Eliz. and Margaret Paine.
3/3/18. Boston, Mass.—Unknown young man.
3/28/18. Lewistown, Mont.—Edward Foster.
3/28/18. Brooklyn, N. Y.—Harry Meyer.
4/2/18. Canton, O.—Wm. Zerbe.
4/2/18. Fremont, O.—Fred K. Bollman, Fred Kolbe.
4/4/18. Athens, Ill.—John W. Rynders.
4/8/18. Reno, Nev.—W. Merriman.
4/9/18. Lincoln, Neb.—C. H. Peter.
4/17/18. Portchester, N. Y.—Louis Dudas.
4/18/18. Van Houten, N. M.—Constantinus Koch.
4/27/18. Anaconda, Mont.—H. C. Lind.
4/29/18. Cleveland, O.—German musician, name unknown.
5/1/18. Camden, N. J.—Harry A. Fay.
5/15/18. Fremont, Neb.—Frank Somejkal.
5/28/18. Paterson, N. J.—George R. Rem.
6/3/18. Williamsport, Pa.—Peter Smabel.
7/18/18. Cincinnati, O.—Unknown man.
7/20/18. Indianapolis, Ind.—Charles C. Hickman.

2. Industrial Causes

Involving primarily the I. W. W.

7/10/17. **Jerome, Ariz.**—**Seventy miners** loaded into cattle cars and sent into California by gunmen of the United Verde Copper Co.

7/12/17. **Bisbee, Ariz.**—**Over 1,000 miners** forcibly deported from their homes to the desert by loyalty league organized by employers. Many deported were I. W. W. members. Officials of the Phelps-Dodge Corporation and other prominent citizens of Bisbee were subsequently indicted but the indictments were later dismissed without trial.

7/23/17. **Aberdeen, S. D.**—**G. J. Bourg,** I. W. W. organizer, seized and taken to jail, later put into an auto with Chief of Police and two others, taken outside of town where mob of business men beat him with clubs while he was held face to the ground.

8/1/17. **Butte, Mont.**—**Frank Little,** member executive board I. W. W. hanged by masked mob until dead.

8/11/17. **Oakland, Cal.**—**I. W. W. headquarters** wrecked by mob of soldiers.

8/22/17. **Duluth, Minn.**—**I. W. W. hall** wrecked by mob of soldiers.

8/29/17. **Franklin, N. J.**—**John Avilla,** I. W. W. organizer, taken in an auto to the woods and hung to a tree by Chief of Police and mob of business men. Cut down when unconscious.

10/4/17. **Stuttgart, Ark.—Luck Laur,** whipped, tarred and feathered and driven out of town for being an I. W. W.

11/9/17. **Tulsa, Okla.—17 I. W. W. prisoners** taken forcibly from the police, beaten, tarred and feathered "in the name of the women and children of Belgium," by mob of citizens and officials calling themselves "The Knights of Liberty."

11/17/17. **Red Lodge, Mont.—Sec'y Finnish I. W. W.,** and several other labor leaders beaten and tortured by mining company representatives, after mock hearing in the court house.

11/28/17. **Red Lodge, Mont.—Emil Koski,** I. W. W. member, beaten by Liberty Committee.

1/5/18. **Seattle, Wash.—Piggott Printing Co.** (printer of Industrial Worker and Seattle Call), plant wrecked by mob of sailors.

2/20/18. **Butte, Mont.—Mell Hathaway,** I. W. W. member, horse-whipped and driven out of town.

3/17/18. **Yerington, Nev.—I. W. W. organizer,** tarred and feathered for "incendiary remarks."

3/9/18. **Yakima, Wash.—H. B. Myers,** Sec'y I. W. W., tarred and feathered.

4/10/18. **Aberdeen, Wash.—Six I. W. W.** leaders tarred, feathered and ordered out of town.

4/13/18. **Muskogee, Okla.—J. A. Lewis,** I. W. W. organizer, taken from jail and deported.

4/15/18. **Jerome, Ariz.—Wm. Waldrop,** I. W. W. organizer, tarred and feathered.

3. Political Causes.

Involving primarily the Non-Partisan League.

10/4/17. **Lake City, Minn.**—Meeting of Non-Partisan League broken up by business men who closed the hall and threatened to play a fire hose on the crowd.

10/19/17. **Rock Creek, Minn.—N. S. Randall** and **Perry Aronson,** Non-Partisan League organizers, kidnapped by mob that threatened to lynch them but released them after deporting them.

1/19/18. **Norwood, Minn.—T. Tharaldson,** Non-Partisan League organizer deported by "loyalty league" mob.

1/19/18. **Jasper, Minn.—Non-Partisan League representative** kidnapped and deported by mob while arranging for a meeting.

1/23/18. **Lakefield, Minn.—Non-Partisan League** meeting broken up by mob composed of county attorney and other officials.

1/25/18. **Akely, Minn.—C. W. Barnes** and **R. R. Hamilton** deported by mob.

2/12/18. **Lakefield, Minn.—James Manahan,** Non-Partisan League attorney, driven out of town.

3/8/18. **Kenyon, Minn.—George Breidel,** N.-P. League organizer, dragged from a moving picture show and put on an outgoing train.

3/23/18. **Rock Creek, Minn.—**Office of **Madelia News,** a League newspaper, painted yellow by a mob.

4/—/18. **New Prague, Minn.—Wm. Wright** painted yellow by mob for League activity.

4/4/18. **Mineola, Texas.—**Several organizers of Non-Partisan League badly beaten and driven out of town.

4/26/18. **Winlock, Wash.—Alfred Knutson** and **W. R. Edwards,** organizers for the Non-Partisan League, tarred and driven out of town.

4/28/18. **Dodge Center, Minn.—**Organizers of the League and farmers who were members driven out of town by a mob.

4/29/18. **Winlock, Wash.—W. R. Edwards,** tarred and driven out of Toledo, near Winlock, second time.

4/29/18. **Sultan, Wash.—Joseph O. Golden,** Non-Partisan League organizer, seized and taken in an auto by young thugs, tarred, feathered and beaten with a revolver.

4/30/18. **Red Wing, Minn.—**Chief witness in the trial of a League organizer driven out of town at point of guns by a mob.

6/—/18. **Madison Lake, Minn.—**Fire hose played by a mob on League parade.

6/—/18. **Rock County, Minn.—**Two farmers that would not renounce League membership driven out of the county. Office of a paper friendly to the League boarded up and editor driven out of the county. One of the deported farmers, John Meents, tarred and feathered upon his return.

6/—/18. **Rock County, Minn.—**Houses and stores of League supporters painted yellow by mob.

6/—/18.—**Pipestone, Minn.—F**armers' co-operative store painted yellow by mob for displaying League candidates' pictures in the window.

6/11/18. **Anoka, Minn.—**A parade of 1,500 League sympathizers broken up by a mob. Many women and children, as well as men, beaten.

6/22/18. **Belle Fourche, S. D.—W. W. Callen,** Non-Partisan League organizer, kidnapped by home guards and taken to another town.

II. CRIMINAL PROSECUTIONS.

1. Espionage Act and Treason Cases.
(Including also cases under act in relation to threats against the President.)

a. Convictions.

(1) For Statements in Private Conversation or Correspondence

12/13/17. **Seattle, Wash.—Louise Olivereau,** Socialist and I. W. W. sympathizer, sentenced to 10 years on several indictments, chargnig interference with the draft.

12/19/17. **Cedar Rapids, Ia.—Joseph Selzer,** I. W. W. organizer, 1 year and $1,000.

12/18/19. **Syracuse, N. Y.—Julie Armbruster** fined $300 for **alleged threats against the President.**

1/17/18. **Parkersburg, W. Va.—Paul Bosko,** Socialist, 15 years for talking against conscription.

1/31/18. **Tacoma, Wash.—J. B. Phelan, Leonard Foster, Wm. Hodges, J. E. Casey, Perry, F. A. Martin and P. Mullen,** I. W. W.'s, five years for alleged disloyal remarks made in conversation. Reversed on appeal and remanded for new trial.

2/24/18. **Van Meter, Ia.—Abe Moore** fined $1,500 on condition that he buy $1,000 worth of Liberty Bonds for alleged attack on Red Cross and recommending resistance to the draft.

3/6/18. **Fargo, N. D.—Henry von Bank** convicted for alleged statement "I would rather see a pair of old trousers flying from the school house flag pole than an American flag." Conviction reversed on appeal.

3/9/18. **Fargo, N. D.—Robert Harden** and **Frank Geizler,** I. W. W.'s, two years for threatening the life of President Wilson.

3/12/18. **St. Louis, Mo.—August Schewing,** one year and one day for alleged seditious remarks.

3/12/18. **St. Louis, Mo.—Wm. H. Schubert** fined $250 for alleged seditious remarks.

3/14/18. **Scranton, Pa.—George Smith,** Socialist, fined $50 for circulating false reports about the Navy.

3/19/18. **Trenton, N. J.—Herman and Nathan Lefkowitz,** Socialists, fined $125 for alleged seditious utterances.

3/21/18. **Burlington, Vt.—Harold Mackley,** 15 years for disloyal remarks.

3/—/18. **Elizabeth, W. Va.—H. E. Kirchner,** State Sec'y of Socialist Party, two years for alleged seditious utterances.

4/5/18. **Toledo, O.—Elias Gracely,** convicted on charge of threatening the President.

4/13/18. **Sioux Falls, S. D.**—**Henry Homan** fined $1,000 for alleged seditious utterances concerning the death of Maj. A. P. Gardner.

4/18/18.—**Lincoln, Neb.**—**Rev. H. M. Hendricksen,** convicted of obstructing recruiting and enlistment.

4/18/18. **Pendleton, Ore.**—**Wm. Isensee,** fined $500, sentenced to 30 days for alleged disloyal remarks to bond-selling committee.

5/2/18. **Dubuque, Ia.**—**Bernard Stenzel,** 18 months and $300 for alleged seditious utterances.

5/3/18. **Milwaukee, Wis.**—**Erwin Schwaer,** 18 months for the alleged remark "President Wilson would be shot within a month."

5/4/18. **Sioux Falls, S. D.**—**Conrad Kornmann,** 10 years and $1,000 fine for opposing the Liberty Loan in a letter to a friend.

5/4/18. **Sioux Falls, S. D.**—**John H. Wolf,** 5 years and $1,000 fine for alleged seditious utterances.

5/6/18. **San Juan, P. R.**—**Gerard Liebisch,** 4 years on a charge of advising drafted men to surrender to the enemy.

5/7/18. **St. Louis, Mo.**—**Frank Strand,** convicted of obsructing recruiting and enlistment by threatening to kill an Austrian who wanted to enlist.

5/7/18. **Charleston, S. C.**—**John Turner,** one year and fined $500 and costs for alleged seditious utterances.

5/7/18. **Charleston, S. C.**—**John Williams,** convicted, sentence postponed, for alleged seditious utterances.

5/9/18. **Rock Island, Ill.**—**Lee Lang,** Socialist, 2 years for violation of the Espionage Act.

5/9/18. **Peoria, Ill.**—**Daniel Mahoney,** 18 months for alleged seditious remarks.

5/10/18. **Oakland, Cal.**—**Otto Janson,** 5 years for saying in effect that the President and U. S. soldiers in France should be shot.

5/16/18. **Aberdeen, S. D.**—**John Bosses,** 2 years and 6 months for threatening the life of the President.

5/16/18. **Aberdeen, S. D.**—**Walter Heynacher,** 5 years for alleged draft obstruction.

5/16/18. **Aberdeen, S. D.**—**Sam Jacobs,** 18 months for alleged seditious remarks.

5/16/18. **Aberdeen, S. D.**—**John Petters,** 1 year and a day for alleged seditious utterances.

5/16/18. **Aberdeen, S. D.**—**Edwin S. Reitz,** 5 years and $1,000 fine for alleged statements tending to obstruct the draft.

5/17/18. **Chicago, Ill.**—**Wm. Eliason,** convicted of alleged seditious utterances.

5/18/18. **Harrisburg, Pa.—John H. Frantz,** 9 months for alleged seditious utterances.

5/19/18. **Sacramento, Cal.—Mrs. C. C. Stemler,** Socialist, 60 days and $150 for alleged seditious remarks.

5/24/18. **New Haven, Conn.—George Kowalsky,** one year and a day for alleged seditious remarks.

5/25/18. **Winona, Minn.—Charles Anding,** 18 months on charge of advising a draftee not to take the federal oath so as not to be sent overseas.

5/28/18. **Pittsburgh, Pa.—John Kolar,** 30 days for alleged seditious remarks.

5/28/18. **New Britain, Conn.—John Kunz,** convicted for the alleged remarks, "Young men are fools to enlist and go across to be blown up" and "Germany had a perfect right to sink the Lusitania."

6/4/18. **Tucson, Ariz.—Wm. Houston.** 3 months for alleged seditious remarks.

6/4/18. **Concord, N. H.—Sidney Mader,** 3 years for alleged seditious utterances.

6/4/18. **Denver, Colo.—J. A. Miller,** 2 years on a charge of telling a young man that he was a fool to fight in this rich man's war and that there was graft in the Red Cross.

6/4/18. **Tucson, Ariz.—Peter Perruchon,** 3 years and $500; **Thomas Martinez,** 2 years and $500, for possessing seditious literature.

6/4/18. **Tucson, Ariz.—August Sandberg,** 2 years and $500 fine for alleged seditious remarks.

6/4/18. **Tucson, Ariz.—G. V. Strode,** 2 years for alleged seditious utterances.

6/4/18. **Concord, N. H.—Gustave H. Taubert,** 3 years for alleged seditious utterances.

6/5/18. **St. Louis, Mo.—Wm. Ehrhardt,** convicted of alleged seditious utterances.

6/6/18. **Hamilton, O.—William Bago,** 15 years for alleged seditious utterances.

6/10/18. **Seattle, Wash.—W. E. Mead,** I. W. W. sympathizer, 5 years for alleged attempts to encourage Canadian troops to desert.

6/26/18. **Zanesville, O.—John Douglas,** 3 years for alleged seditious remarks cursing the United States.

6/26/18. **Columbus, O.—Edward A. Kolbe,** 5 years for alleged seditious remarks.

6/27/18. **Sacramento, Cal.—Miss Myra Dunton,** Socialist, 40 days and $10 fine for alleged seditious utterances.

6/27/18. **Portland, Ore.—Gustav Erdtmann,** an I. W. W. convicted under espionage act for telling lumbermen to leave the Loyal Legion of Loggers and Lumbermen and to join the I. W. W. if they wanted results.

6/30/18. **Sacramento, Cal.—Carl Schilter,** 2½ years and $200 for alleged seditious remarks.

7/4/18. **Tucson, Ariz.—Curt von Einem,** convicted on five counts for alleged seditious remarks.

7/15/18. **Tonopah, Nev.—Al Shidler, Socialist,** 2 years and $100 fine for alleged seditious utterances.

7/1718. **Detroit, Mich.—Frank Monparler,** 18 months for alleged seditious remarks.

7/10/18. **Columbus, O.—A. F. W. Benzin,** 4½ years for alleged seditious remarks.

7/20/18. **Los Angeles, Cal.—L. N. Legendre,** 2 years for saying, "This is a war fostered by Morgan and the rich."

7/18/18. **New York, N. Y.—Arthur Roth,** 5 years for alleged seditious statements in an intercepted letter to a friend.

7/24/18. **Detroit, Mich.—Wm. Powell,** 20 years and $10,000 for alleged remarks to the effect that the government was a lie throughout, that German barbarities were only fiction, that the Germans were right in sinking the Lusitania, that Germany would wipe the Allies off the earth in three years.

7/28/18. **Cincinnati, O.—Fred Bisdorf,** convicted of alleged pro-German utterances.

8/7/18. **Cincinnati, O.—Clark Dickson,** convicted on three counts for alleged seditious remarks.

8/8/18. **Detroit, Mich.—Anthony C. Stopa** and **Albert Feiron,** 20 years and $10,000 each for alleged seditious utterances.

8/8/18. **Newark, N. J.—Charles Ohlsen,** convicted of alleged seditious utterances.

8/13/18. **Tacoma, Wash.—W. H. Kaufman,** single taxer and grange leader, 5 years for the alleged remarks, "Liberty bonds are a disgrace to America" and "America was buncoed into the war by munition makers."

8/17/18. **Cleveland, O.—Fred J. Saal,** 10 years for alleged seditious utterances.

9/—/18. **Enid, Okla.—F. M. Darby,** 3 months and $300 fine for alleged seditious utterances.

9/—/18. **Cincinnati, O.—C. B. Schoberg,** convicted of alleged seditious utterances.

9/2/18. **Minneapolis, Minn.—John C. Seebach,** 18 months and $3,000 for alleged remarks tending to discourage enlistment.

9/6/18. **Cincinnati, O.—Henry Feltman,** convicted of alleged seditious utterances. **J. C. Masten** pleaded guilty to same charge.

9/7/18. **Cincinnati, O.—J. Henry Kruse,** convicted of alleged seditious utterances.

9/18/18. **Syracuse, N. Y.—John A. Tolishus,** 1 year and 3

months and $100 on five counts for alleged seditious utterances.

9/23/18. **Lincoln, Neb.—Mack Denny,** 30 days for alleged threats against the President.

9/23/18. **Lincoln, Neb.—Frank Hockbarth,** 4 months for alleged seditious utterances.

9/25/18. **New Haven, Conn.—Ludwig Evanicki,** 1 year and a day for alleged seditious remarks.

9/25/18. **Portland, Ore.—Theodore Olson,** 2 years for alleged disloyalty.

9/25/18. **New Haven, Conn.—Charles Sahrbacher,** 1 year and a day for alleged seditious remarks.

9/29/18. **Enid, Okla.—Rev. W. M. Hicks,** 20 years for alleged disloyalty.

10/4/18. **Concord, N. H.—Fred Steadman,** 2 years for violation of the Espionage Act.

10/16/18. **Amarillo, Tex.—Mrs. Flora Foreman,** Socialist, 5 years for alleged seditious utterances.

10/22/18. **Newark, N. J.—Hugo Steidle,** 3 months for alleged seditious remarks.

10/2318. **Oregon City, Ore.—P. W. Meredith,** convicted on a charge of seditious utterances.

11/1/18. **Chicago, Ill.—August Weissenfels,** 10 years for opposing his son's enlistment in the army.

11/9/18. **Omaha, Neb.—L. W. Boehner,** convicted of violation of the Espionage Act.

11/18/18. **St. Louis, Mo.—Wm. F. Wehmeyer,** $1000, **Wm. P. Elmer,** $1000, **Wm. A. Brackett,** $150, **August Wiess,** $200, **Claude Bunyard,** $200, **J. C. Klein,** $400, for alleged disloyal utterances.

11/—/18. **Auburn, N. Y.—John S. Randolph,** sentenced to 10 years in prison for alleged seditious remarks.

12/7/18. **Providence, R. I.—Dr. Frederick O. Balcom,** 1 year for alleged seditious utterances.

12/11/18. **El Paso, Tex.—Edgar Held,** convicted of violation of the Espionage Act.

12/12/18. **Auburn, N. Y.—Max Machner,** 7 months for alleged seditious utterances.

12/14/18. **Omaha, Neb.—Tom Kerl,** fined $2,000 and costs for alleged seditious remarks.

2/5/19. **Portland, Ore.—J. Henry Albers,** President of one of the largest flour-milling corporations on Pacific Coast convicted for alleged seditious statements said to have been provoked by a business competitor.

(2) Convictions for Statements in Public
Addresses or Public Print.

10/—/17. **St. Louis, Mo.—Frank A. Feldman,** 3 months for alleged remarks tending to obstruct the draft.

10/4/17. **Davenport, Iowa.—Daniel H. Wallace,** ex-British

soldier and radical, 20 years for a speech on conscription and the war. Went insane and died in jail.

10/22/17. **Trenton, N. J.—Frederick Krafft,** former Socialist candidate for Governor, 5 years and $1,000 for criticism of conscription in a street corner speech.

10/26/17. **Mankato, Minn.—A. L. Sugarman,** State Secretary Socialist Party, 3 years for a speech about conscrpition.

10/31/17. **St. Louis, Mo.—Thomas Cornell,** Socialist, 2 years for a speech calculated to interfere with recruiting.

12/1/17. **San Juan, P. R.—Vincente Balbas Capo,** 8 years and $4,000 fine for an editorial in his paper as to drafting of Porto Ricans who had declined United States citizenship.

12/18/17. **Fargo, N. D.—Kate Richards O'Hare,** 5 years for "discouraging enlistments." See pamphlet published by N. C. L. B. Appealed, U. S. Circuit Court of Appeals.

3/8/18. **St. Louis, Mo.—A. H Steinbeck,** editor of "Republican Headlight," fined $200 for an alleged seditious editorial.

4/5/18. **Marinette, Wis.—Rev. C. H. Auerswald,** fined $100 and costs for seditious utterances.

4/19/18. **Minneapolis, Minn.—J. O. Bentall,** Socialist candidate for Governor, and J. A. Peterson, candidate for Republican nomination for United States Senate, sentenced to 5 and 4 years, respectively, for speeches and articles during their campaign activities.

4/30/18. **Los Angeles, Cal.—Robert Goldstein,** 10 years and $5,000 for producing film "Spirit of '76" disparaging the British Government.

4/30/18. **Kansas City, Mo.—Carl Glesser,** 5 years for publishing alleged seditious articles in the Missouri Staats Zeitung.

5/4/18. **Minneapolis, Minn.—E. A. Engelin,** 5 years for alleged attempt to incite mutiny and obstruct enlistments in a speech.

5/9/18. **Peoria, Ill.—C. H. Kamann,** 3 years and $5,000 for making alleged seditious remarks to children in his history class.

5/13/18. **Greenville, S. C.—W. P. Beard,** 1 year and $500 for alleged seditious statements in his paper, "The Scimitar."

6/1/18. **Kansas City, Mo.—Mrs. Rose Pastor Stokes,** Socialist, 10 years for writing a signed communication to the Kansas City Star about a speech delivered by her on the government and profiteering.

6/6/18. **Oklahoma City, Okla.—Orville C. Enfield,** Socialist, 20 years and $500 for alleged seditious utterances.

6/10/18. **Boston, Mass.—John J. Ballam,** Socialist, 1 year for saying in effect that working men should not go to war because they would be required to kill other workingmen in different uniforms.

6/21/18. **Brooklyn, N. Y.—Joseph F. Rutherford, Wm. E. Van Armburgh, R. J. Martin, Fred H. Robison, A. H. McMillan, G. H. Fisher, C. H. Woodworth,** each 20 years for publication and distribution of "The Finished Mystery" and for the activities of the International Bible Students Association. **Giovanni de Cecca,** sentence deferred pending investigation; on 7/11/18 received 10 years.

6/28/18. **Cleveland O.—A. L. Hitchcock,** Socialist school commissioner, 10 years for alleged remarks against the Liberty Loan in a speech at Sandusky on April 6.

6/29/18. **Kansas City, Mo.—Jacob Frohwerk,** 10 years for writing alleged seditious articles for the Missouri Staats Zeitung.

7/6/18. **Providence, R. I.—Joseph M. Coldwell,** state organizer of the Socialist Party, 3 years for alleged seditious statements in a speech.

7/19/18. **Los Angeles, Cal.—Ricardo Magon and Librado Rivera,** 20 and 15 years, respectively, for alleged seditious statements in a Mexican anarchist newspaper.

8/6/18. **Cleveland, O.—Rev. Manasses C. Bontrager,** Amish Mennonite bishop, fined $500 for an article deploring the buying of Liberty Bonds.

8/11/18. **Cleveland, O.—Rev. W. A. Werth,** two years for alleged statement made at a soldier's funeral that the army was rotten with foul disease.

9/11/18. **Cleveland, O.—Eugene V. Debs,** former Socialist candidate for president, 10 years for alleged seditious remarks in a speech at Canton, O.

9/17/18. **Buffalo, N. Y.—Wm. Dodge,** Socialist Labor Party member, six years for alleged seditious remarks.

10/18/18. **Davenport, Ia.—Dr. W. C. Matthey,** convicted of "aiding and abetting Daniel H. Wallace in wilfully obstructing the enlistment or recruiting service of the United States."

11/21/18. **Chicago, Ill.—Rev. David Gerdes,** a Dunkard, 10 years for alleged seditious sermon.

11/21/18. **Chicago, Ill.—John D. Manus,** 3 years for alleged seditious letters to newspapers.

12/6/18. **Philadelphia, Pa.—Joseph V. Stilson,** secretary, 3 years and Joseph Sukys, business manager of Lithuanian Socialpaper Kova, 3 months for publishing alleged seditious matter.

12/30/18. **Philadelphia, Pa.—Martin Darkon** and **Louis Werner,** editors of the Philadelphia Tageblatt, each 5 years; Herman Lemke, business manager, 2 years; and **Peter Schaefer,** president, and **Paul Vogel,** treasurer, each 1 year; for alleged pro-German editorials.

12/31/18. **Portland, Oregon—Dr. Mary Equi,** Socialist and

I. W W. sympathizer, 3 years and $500 fine on a charge of violating the Espionage Act.

1/9/19. **Chicago, Ill.—Victor L. Berger, Adolph Germer, J. Louis Engdahl, Irwin St. John Tucker** and **Wm. F. Kruse,** heads of Socialist Party, convicted under Espionage Act and sentenced to 20 years each for their activities as speakers and writers for the Socialist Party.

1/20/19. **Brooklyn, N. Y.—Morris Zucker, Socialist,** 15 years for alleged seditious utterances in a Socialist speech.

Portland, Ore.—Floyd Ramp, convicted for alleged seditious statements.

Newark, N. J.—Benedict Preith and his fellow editors convicted for alleged seditious articles in a German-lauguage newspaper.

Madison, Wis.—Louis B. Nagler convicted for alleged statements against the Red Cross, Y. M. C. A., etc.

(3) Convictions for Distributing Literature.

6/16/17. **Topeka, Kan.—I. T. Boutell,** Socialist, 6 months for distributing leaflets "A Good Soldier," by Jack London, to drafted men.

11/2/17. **Sioux Falls, S. D.—Emanuel Baltzer and 26 Socialists** sentenced from 1 to 2 years for circulating a petition charging unfair administration of the draft. Conviction set aside by U. S. Supreme Court upon filing of a confession of error by the attorney general and cases remanded to lower court.

11/2/17. **Sioux Falls, S. D.—Wm. J. Head,** State Socialist Secretary, sentenced to 3 years and $500 fine for circulating a petition for the repeal of the draft law. Conviction set aside by United States Supreme Court upon filing of a confession of error by the attorney general and case remanded to lower court.

11/17/17. **Albany, N. Y.—Clinton Pierce, et al,** 4 Socialists, convicted for distributing leaflet, "The Price We Pay."

12/21/17. **Philadelphia, Pa.—Charles T. Schenck and Dr. Eliz. Baer,** Socialists, convicted of conspiracy for distributing pamphlet relative to the Draft Act.

1/11/18. **Denver, Colo.—Perley Doe, Socialist,** 18 months for circulating chain letter criticising the accuracy of statement that the war was brought on by Germany's breaking her pledges.

1/—/18. **Des Moines, Iowa.—D. T. Blodgett,** 20 years for circulating leaflet opposing the re-election of Congressmen who voted for conscription.

2/12/18. **Parkersburg, W. Va.—Floyd Teter, Alman J. Stainaker and Fred E. Thompson,** each fined $10,000 and costs for conspiracy to obstruct recruiting and enlistment in publishing and distributing an alleged seditious article.

3/21/18. **Burlington, Vt.—Rev. C. H. Waldron,** 15 years for distributing an alleged seditious article.

5/6/18. **San Juan, P. R.—Florencio Romero,** 4 years for circulating anti-draft literature and attempting to form an anti-militarist league.

5/28/18. **Pittsburgh, Pa.—J. G. Shellenberger,** 5 months for opposing Liberty Bonds and circulating a seditious pamphlet.

6/6/18. **Seattle, Wash.—Emil Herman,** State Secretary, Socialist party, 10 years for alleged obstruction of recruiting in having printed and distributed circulars entitled, "Don't Be a Soldier, Be a Man."

7/10/18. **Seattle, Wash.—Frank Shaffer,** 2½ years for alleged circulation of "The Finished Mystery."

7/11/18. **Providence, R. I.—Emil Yanyar,** Socialist, convicted of conveying false information tending to obstruct recruiting and enlistment in distributing circulars stating that 10,000 men in the state and 4,000 men in Providence had refused to register.

10/26/18. **New York, N. Y.—Hyman Rozansky** (turned State's evidence), 3 years; **Jacob Abrahms, Samuel Lippman** and **Hyman Lachowsky,** each 20 years and $1000; and **Mollie Steimer,** 15 years and $500 for publishing and circulating a revolutionary pamphlet denouncing intervention in Russia. **J. Schwarz,** also indicted, died in prison before coming to trial.

2/19/19. **New York, N. Y.—American Socialist Society** convicted under the Espionage Act for publishing Scott Nearing's pamphlet, "The Great Madness." The same jury acquitted Nearing, although it was admitted that he wrote the pamphlet.

Brooklyn, N. Y.—Stephen Binder, convicted of preparing to circulate a book of alleged seditious character.

(b) Indictments Found, Trial Pending or Result Unknown.

11/—/17. **Sioux Falls, S. D.—Former U. S. Senator R. F. Pettigrew,** indicted under the Espionage Act for writing in opposition to war.

11/—/17. **St. Louis, Mo.—C. J. Henninger and A. Jablowsky,** indicted for attributing sordid motives to people eager for war.

11/24/17. **New York, N. Y.—Jeremiah A. O'Leary,** advocate of Irish freedom, and others, indicted for conspiracy to violate the Espionage Act.

12/—/17. **Hilland, S. D.—Fred Fairchild,** indicted under Espionage Act for stating in argument that he would refuse to serve if drafted.

1/28/18. **Kansas City, Kan.—Dr. Adolph Koerber,** arrested on indictment alleging seditious utterances.

2/13/18. **Johnson City, Tenn.—Will Martin,** Socialist, indicted for seditious remarks.

3/5/18. **Fargo, N. D.—J. H. Wishek,** indicted for alleged remark that "banks having large holdings of Liberty Bonds are unsafe for people to keep their money in."

3/20/18. **Withita, Kan.—Henry M. Schultz,** indicted under Espionage Act for alleged seditious utterances.

4/1/18. **Lincoln, Neb.—Rev. Hiltner,** indicted for alleged remark "the German emperor is right. Might makes right. America had no business entering the war."

4/3/18. **Monroe, La.—Sarah Story,** 76 years old, indicted for distributing "The Finished Mystery." **Fred Gaebler** indicted for alleged seditious utterances.

4/10/18. **Lincoln, Neb.—G. H. Smidt,** indicted for alleged seditious remarks.

4/12/18. **Syracuse, N. Y.—Oscar Oschner,** Russellite, indicted under Espionage Act for selling "The Finished Mystery."

4/17/18. **Cape Girardeau, Mo.—Rev. M. D. Collins, Rev. E. C. Shutt and Wm. Wagner,** indicted for alleged disloyal utterances.

4/23/18. **Richmond, Ky.—David M. Meyers,** indicted for alleged disloyalty and draft obstruction.

4/28/18. **Phoenix, Ariz.—Ed McNally,** pleaded not guilty to indictment for alleged disloyal remarks.

5/15/18. **Los Angeles, Cal.—Mrs. Clara Gutormse,** indicted under Espionage Act for alleged hostile reception to Red Cross solicitor.

6/26/18. **Helena, Mont.—Ned Munley and Wm. Metzdorf,** indicted for alleged seditious utterances.

7/10/18. **Cleveland, O.—J. S. Switensky, Wasil Sawczyn** and **Paul Ladan,** I. W. W.'s, editors of a Ukrainian paper, Robytnik, indicted for publishing an article tending to interfere with the prosecution of the war.

7/—/18. **Minneapolis, Minn.—Albert Steinhauser** indicted for publishing extracts from German papers, most of which had been published in New York Times and passed by Press Cable Censor at New York.

7/29/18. **Seattle, Wash.—George Michel, Leon Rubio, T. A. Montgomery, M. M. Jones, S. M. Brandau and Walter Barrett,** I. W. W.'s, indicted for alleged seditious utterances.

8/7/18. **Cincinnati, O.—C. H. Wagner, C. B. Schoberg, J. H. Kruse, Henry Feltman, Matt Felton, Herman Rawe,** indicted for alleged seditious utterances.

9/—/18. **Wenatchee, Wash.—H. Witter,** indicted for violation of the Espionage Act.

9/24/18. **New York, N. Y.—A. I. Shiplacoff** and **John Reed,** Socialists, indicted for alleged disloyal language about the Army and Navy in opposition to intervention in Russia at a Socialist meeting on September 13, 1918.

10/10/18. **Fargo, N. D.—Walter T. Mills,** indicted for alleged seditious utterances in a Non-Partisan League speech.

10/18/18. **Salt Lake City, Utah.—Joe Rogers,** secretary I. W. W. indicted on charge alleging circulation of incendiary literature calling for a general strike.

10/26/18. **Great Falls, Mont.—Mike Milosh,** indicted under the Espionage Act.

10/29/18. **Milwaukee, Wis.—Victor Berger, E. T. Melms, Oscar Ameringer, Louis Arnold and Eliz. Thomas,** all prominent Socialists, indicted under the Espionage Act.

10/29/18. **Milwaukee, Wis.—Alexander Klug, Chas. Engels, Ed Enders and A. H. Wernicke,** indicted under the Espionage Act for alleged seditious remarks.

10/30/18. **Milwaukee, Wis.—John C. Kleist, Otto Pergande** and Carl Schultz, indicted for alleged seditious remarks.

12/15/18. **New Orleans, La.—T. C. Coats,** indicted under Espionage Act, for alleged seditious letter.

(c) Acquittals and Disagreements in Espionage Act, Draft Act and Treason Cases.

7/11/17. **Baltimore, Md.—R. E. Baker** and **J. M. Wilhide,** Socialists, acquitted of violation of Section 3 of the Espionage Act in distributing "The Price We Pay" at a recruiting meeting.

10/18/17. **Grand Rapids, Mich.—Adolph Germer et al,** acquitted on charge of conspiracy to violate the draft act in circulating "The Price We Pay," and the Socialist Party "Proclamation and War Program."

10/25/17. **Louisville, Ky.—Edmund Groeschl,** acquitted of violation of Espionage Act in distributing Socialist Labor Party leaflet about conscription.

10/—/17. **Bay City, Mich.—John Peterson,** Socialist, acquitted of violation of Espionage Act, for wearing button inscribed "Not a dollar, not a man for war."

1/27/18. **Butte, Mont.—Ves Hall,** acquitted of violation of Espionage Act in cursing the President.

2/9/18. **Denver, Colo.—Orlando Hitt,** acquitted of charge of seditious utterances in private conversation.

21518. **Brooklyn, N. Y.—Paul Hennig,** acquitted of charge of treason for alleged tampering with torpedo gyroscope parts.

2/21/18. **Tacoma, Wash.—Frank Bostrom,** acquitted of violation of Espionage Act, in selling Wallace's book "Shanghaied in the European War."

3/14/18. **Indianapolis, Ind.—13 Montenegrins** acquitted by direction of judge, of conspiracy to violate draft.

3/19/18. **Indianapolis, Ind.—Joseph Zimmerman,** Socialist, acquitted of charge of violation of Espionage Act by seditious utterances in a public speech advocating the withdrawal of the United States from the war.

3/23/18. **Baltimore, Md.—Edw. Otis,** Russian sailor, acquitted of charge of tampering with steering gear of ship.

3/26/18. **Philadelphia, Pa.—Adolph Werner** and **Martin Darkow,** editors of Philadelphia "Tageblatt," acquitted on charge of treason, based on alleged pro-German editorials.

4/—/18. **Shreveport, La.—State Senator S. J. Harper,** acquitted of wilfully interfering with military forces in distributing pamphlet.

4//18. **Houston, Tex.—Charles Meitzen,** acquitted on charge of printing articles in violation of the Espionage Act.

4/13/18. **Kansas City, Kan.—Eva Harding** and several other Socialists acquitted of conspiracy to violate the Draft Act.

5/24/18. **Los Angeles, Cal.—Joe Beayans,** acquitted of violation of Espionage Act in making alleged seditious remarks.

5/24/18. **Denver, Colo.—W. B. Tanner,** acquitted on ten counts of violation of the Espionage Act in remarks made in various conversations.

6/11/18. **Paterson, N. J.—H. J. Rubenstein,** W. I. I. U. organizer, acquitted on a charge of alleged seditious utterances.

6/24/18. **Wilmington, Del.—Frank Stephens,** single taxer, acquitted of violation of Espionage Law in making alleged seditious remarks to a Liberty Loan saleswoman.

6/—/18. **Detroit, Mich.—Louis Jasick,** acquitted on a charge of threatening the president.

7/6/18. **St. Louis, Mo.—Dr. Chas. H. Weinsberg,** acquitted of violation of Espionage Act in statements on the war situation made in newspaper interviews in St. Louis Post Dispatch.

7/13/18. **Hartford, Con.—Herman Schurer,** acquitted on charge of alleged seditious utterances.

7/24/18. **Birmingham, Ala.—Pete Youngman,** acquitted of violation of Espionage Act.

7/26/18. **Los Angeles, Cal.—E. K. Brooks,** acquitted on charge of calling the flag "a dirty rag."

7/28/18. **Birmingham, Ala—Wm. A. Denson,** prominent attorney, acquitted of violation of the Espionage Act in making alleged seditious utterances.

10/5/18. **New York, N. Y.—Max Eastman, Floyd Dell, C.**

Merrill Rogers, Arthur Young and John Reed, Socialists, tried for the second time for publishing articles and cartoons in "The Masses" interfering with enlistments. Jury disagreed again. Indictments later dismissed.

10/12/18. **Jenera, O.—Rev. John Gauss,** acquitted of interfering with the draft.

11/13/18. **St. Louis, Mo.—H. C. Koenig,** acquitted on charge of alleged disloyal remarks about the Red Cross ,the Y. M. C. A. and the president.

11/15/18. **Little Rock, Ark.—J. H. Ward,** acquitted of violation of Espionage Act.

11/27/18. **Mt. Vernon, N. Y.—Dr. G. C. Weiss,** acquitted on charge of alleged seditious utterances.

12/13/18. **New Orleans, La.—Julius B. Gerdes,** acquitted on charge of writing seditious remarks on his questionnaire.

12/14/18. **Minneapolis, Minn.—J. V. Free,** Non-Partisan League organizer, acquitted of violation of the Espionage Act.

12/17/18. **Milwaukee, Wis.—Julius Henning,** acquitted of violation of Espionage Act.

2/19/19. **New York, N. Y.—Scott Nearing** acquitted of alleged violation of the Espionage Act by writing "The Great Madness."

(2) Obstructing the Draft Act.

6/15/17. **Orofino, Idaho.—Edw. Hofstede,** in jail five months before trial, sentenced to 4 months on charge of advising young men not to register.

6/—/17. **Columbus, Ohio.—A. A. Hennacy** and **H. E. Townsley,** 2 years for advising refusal to register.

7/12/17. **Charles Philips** and **Owen Cattell,** $500 and 1 day for conspiring to violate the draft law.

7/21/17. **Cleveland, O.—C. E. Ruthenberg, C. Baker** and **A. Wagenknecht,** 1 year for inducing men not to register. Supreme Court affirmed sentence 1/15/18.

10/12/17. **Freeport, Ill.—James Cully,** convicted of inciting reciting resistance to conscription.

10/23/17. **New York, N. Y.—C. R. Cheyney** and **L. C. Fraina,** 30 days each for conspiracy to violate Draft Act, by remarks made in public meeting on conscientious objectors. Appealed.

10/23/17. **Minneapolis, Minn.—J. O. Bental,** active Socialist, sentenced to 1 year for advising men not to register.

10/—/17. **Cincinnati, Ohio.—16 Socialists** indicted for conspiracy for advising men not to register.

11/3/17. **Wheelng, Va.—Edwin Firth, Hilton Bias, Ben Green** and **Henry Howes,** 6 months and costs for conspiracy to defraud the government by circulating literature opposed to the draft.

1/15/18. **New York, N. Y. Emma Goldman** and **Alexander Berkman,** sentenced to 2 years and $10,000 fine for conspiracy to violate conscription act, upheld by U. S. Supreme Court. Same decision applies to **L. Kramer** and **M. Becker,** who refused to register on ground of unconstitutionality of Draft Act.

1/17/18. **San Francisco, Cal—Daniel O'Connell,** 2 years for violating draft law. Appealed.

3/19/18. **Seattle, Wash.—Hulet M. Wells, Sam Sadler, Joe** and **Morris Pass,** 2 years each for seditious conspiracy to obstruct draft.

3/27/18. **Springfield, Ill.—Mr. and Mrs. Fadoo Meyers,** 90 days each for advising their sons not to register.

5/28/18. **Pittsburgh, Pa.—John Katkus,** 10 days for an alleged attempt to obstruct recruiting and enlisment.

6/11/18. **Philadelphia, Pa.—Harry Fadel,** 1 year for tearing up his questionnaire.

10/30/18. **New York, N. Y.—Roger N. Baldwin,** 1 year for refusing to take physical examination.

10/18/18. **Mineola, L. I.—Alex M. Benecke, Pincus Strul** and **William Norocki,** 1 year for refusal to register.

(3) Convictions Under State and Local Laws.

4/3/17. **New York, N. Y.—Stephen Kerr,** Socialist Labor Party member, 3 months for disorderly conduct in making a speech on Madison Square.

4/4/17. **New York, N. Y.—Henry Jager, Socialist,** 3 months for speaking in Madison Square.

4/4/17. **New York.—I. Meirowitz and Deutsch,** Socialists, each fined $10 in connection with a meeting in Madison Square.

4/-19/17. **New York, N. Y.—George L. Glison,** Socialist, 6 months for distributing an anti-war pamphlet.

5/19/17. **New York, N. Y.—Harry Aurin,** Socialist, fined $10 for distributing anti-conscription circulars.

7/12/17. **New York, N. Y.—Hyman Nemser** and **Meyer Leitzes,** Socialists, each fined $10 for street speaking and distributing Socialist leaflets, respectively.

8/24/17. **New York, N. Y.—John Hehir,** fined $15 on a charge of trampling on the flag.

8/31/17. **New York, N. Y.—Bertha Frazer,** Socialist, fined $50 for alleged seditious remarks in a street-corner speech.

8/31/17. **New York, N. Y.—Hyman Levinson,** Socialist, 30

days for the alleged remark, "Kaiser Wilson has declared war for Morgan and Rockefeller."

9/—/17. **New York, N. Y. Jacob Frachter,** Socialist, 6 months for alleged remarks against conscription in a street speech.

9/—/17. **New York, N. Y.—Alfred Levitt,** Socialist, 20 days for street speech urging repeal of conscription.

9/13/17. **New York, N. Y.—Richard Mackenzie,** fined $15 for disorderly conduct for speaking in the street though exonerated of making seditious utterances.

9/28/17. **Two Harbors, Minn.—Allan S. Broms,** Socialist, of St. Paul, 90 days for utterances attacking the war, constituting disorderly conduct.

Bemidji, Minn.—Jesse Dunning, I. W. W., 2 years for having E. G. Flynn's and Emile Pouget's book on sabotage on sale.

10/12/17. **Seattle, Wash.—Ole Olson,** 30 days and $100 for alleged seditious utterances in a street-corner sermon.

11/7/17. **Chicago, Ill.—George Thulpape,** fined $50 and costs for alleged remarks to the effect that President Wilson was no good and the United States is going to lose the war.

11/10/17. **Atlantic, Ia.—W. Theo. Woodward,** 6 months and $600 for belonging to the People's Council, a violation of a state law. Prison sentence suspended.

11/12/17. **Duluth, Minn.—Scott Nearing and 3 others** arrested for vagrancy during raid on People's Council meeting. Nearing fined $50 and others acquitted.

11/17/17. **New York, N. Y.—Nathan Levine,** Socialist, 1 year and 20 days for the alleged remark that he would rather go to prison than be drafted for the army.

11/30/17. **Faribault, Minn.—E. B. Ford, Eliz. Ford,** Socialist Labor Party members, and **Ed Bosky,** $500 and 1 year for "discouraging enlistment" by editorial in their paper.

12/1/17. **New York, N. Y.—Adolph Cabet,** Socialist, 30 days for alleged remarks against Liberty bonds in a street speech.

12/7/17. **Louisville, Ky.—Richard Schell,** aged and infirm German, fined $5 (suspended) for alleged disloyal remarks.

12/8/7. **Los Angeles, Cal.—Robert Whitaker, Floyd Hardin** and **Harold Story,** sentenced to 6 months and an aggregate fine of $1,200 for unlawful assembly in connection with Christian Pacifist Conference. See pamphlet published by N. C. L. B. Decision reversed by Appellate Court.

12/8/17. **Portland, Ore.—J. M. Beck,** a Socialist, $50 and 20 days in jail for distributing a pamphlet without a license.

12/20/17. **Mankato, Minn.—Frank J. Busch,** $500 for alleged seditious remarks. At suggestion of the judge he bought

$1,000 Liberty Bonds and subscribed $100 to the Red Cross and $50 each, to the Y. M. C. A. and K. of C.

12/20/17. **Grass Valley, Cal.—Gus Swift,** 60 days for disturbing the peace by making seditious remarks.

12/28/17. **San Francisco, Cal.—Alexander Horr,** Socialist, 6 months for disorderly conduct in connection with Scott Nearing meeting.

1/1/18. **Greenwich, Conn.—Fleming Jordan,** 6 months (suspended) and $25 and costs for alleged breach of peace in speaking disrespectfully of the President.

1/2/18. **Media, Pa.—M. Logeda and Wm. Derman,** Russian Socialists, guilty under Civil War statute of inciting to riot, resisting arrest and preaching against the President and Congress.

1/2/18. **Bayonne, N. J.—John Seaford,** 6 months on a charge of spitting on the flag.

1/11/18. **Fairmont, Minn.—Walter Meyers,** $200 for alleged remark that the United States never could whip the Kaiser and had no business sending troops or food to Europe.

1/11/18. **Nome, Alaska.—Bruce Rogers,** Socialist, convicted of violation of territorial sedition act for printing "We must make the world safe for democracy if we have to 'bean' the Goddess of Liberty to do it."

1/20/18. **Muskogee, Okla.—Fred Baker,** Socialist, convicted of making derogatory remarks about his country.

1/26/18. **Philadelphia, Pa.—Casper Oberstadt,** 30 days and $150 fine, **Louis Abrahamson, Isadore Axelrod, Walter A. Ebbits** and **Solomon Bold,** Socialists, each 15 days and $150 fine for distribution of anti-conscription leaflets.

2/—/18. **Yerington, Nev.—Peter Slaugh,** Socialist, $15 and costs for "loud talking" in connection with alleged seditious remarks.

2/8/18. **Milwaukee, Wis.—Wilhelm L. Sixtus,** fined $25 and costs for disorderly conduct in rejoicing at the sinking of the Tuscania.

2/11/18. **Alexandria, Minn.—Carl A. Wold,** editor of Park Region "Echo," 3 months and $200 for seditious editorial.

2/11/18. **Milwaukee, Wis.—Fred Young,** fined $25 and costs for alleged seditious remarks.

2/12/18. **Lakefield, Minn.—Joseph Gilbert,** secretary Non-Partisan League, 3 months on charge of unlawful assemblage.

2/21/18. **Bayonne, N. J.—Miss Rose Weiner,** fined $50 for an alleged remark to the effect that she was glad the Tuscania was sunk and hoped that other transports meet a like fate.

2/26/18. **St. Paul, Minn.—A. C. Townley** and **Jos. Gilbert,** president and secretary of Non-Partisan League, indicted for circulating pamphlets "tending to discourage enlistments." Gilbert sentenced to one year. Reversed on appeal.

2/27/18. **Pipestone, Minn.—G. D. Brewer,** Non-Partisan League lecturer, 60 days and $100 fine for "unlawful assemblage."

3/8/18. **Milwaukee, Wis.—Anton Sudniki** fined $25 for alleged seditious remarks.

3/9/18. **Niagara Falls, N. Y.—Stanley Lindenberg,** secretary Socialist Local, 6 months for having "defied, cast contempt upon and defiled the flag of the United States."

3/12/18. **Chicago, Ill.—J. W. Beckstrom,** fined $50 for refusing to stand when "Star Spangled Banner" was played in the theatre.

3/13/18. **New York, N. Y.—Herman Singer,** 5 days for union agitation among workers in a munition factory.

3/15/18. **Fergust Falls, Minn.—Henry Stock,** 3 months for alleged remark that he "wished the Germans had gotten the whole bunch of American soldiers aboard the Tuscania."

3/19/18. **Passaic, N. J.—John Mathewski,** fined $100 for disloyal utterances.

3/28/18. **Fresno, Cal.—Fred Mindinger,** 30 days for alleged seditious utterances.

3/28/18. **New York, N. Y.—Mrs. Mary Tekah,** 6 months for flying a German flag from her window.

3/29/18. **Brooklyn, N. Y.—John Ferlan,** 3 months for alleged seditious utterances.

3/29/18. **Hoboken, N. J.—Joseph Reik,** 1 year for alleged remark, "I hope every ——————— ——————— is drowned before he gets to the other side. They are only a bunch of dirty bums.

3/30/18. **Baltimore, Md.—Henry Anbelsen,** a Danish sailor, 2 months for alleged seditious utterances.

4/—/18. **Townsend, Mont.—Albert E. Maken,** 4 to 8 years for alleged seditious utterances.

4/—/18. **Deer Lodge, Mont.—August A. Miller,** 2 to 4 years for alleged seditious utterances.

4/1/**Hoboken, N. J.—Fred Povik,** 1 year for alleged seditious utterances.

4/1/18. **Hoboken, N. J.—Stanley Rabitz,** 1 year for alleged seditious utterances.

4/4/18. **Los Angeles, Cal.—Sam Jesky,** 90 days for alleged seditious utterances.

4/8/18. **New York, N. Y.—Herman Elsmer,** 90 days for alleged seditious remarks against the President.

4/10/18. **New York, N. Y.—Henry Schneider,** 6 months for sneering at Liberty Loan.

4/16/18. **Missoula, Mont.—Pete Ervik,** two to four years for alleged seditious utterances.

4/16/18. **Helena, Mont.—John Ruck,** 3 to 6 years for the alleged remark that he hoped the Germans would sink every ship America sends to Europe.

4/17/18. **Fremont, Neb.—John Hauer,** 20 years for alleged seditious remarks.

4/18/18. **Sedalia, Mo.—Fred Esser,** 6 months for alleged seditious remarks.

4/20/18. **Lewistown, Mont.—John Harrington,** 2 to 4 years for alleged statement that he hoped the Kaiser would beat the American army and sink our transports.

4/29/18. **Minneapolis, Minn.—Rev. August Doeppling** fined $500 for alleged seditious utterances.

5/2/18. **Monroe, La.—Miss Ronda M. Hendricks,** $300 or 6 months for alleged seditious remarks.

5/7/18. **Red Wing, Minn.—N. S. Randall,** Non-Partisan League organizer, four months and $250 for alleged disloyal utterances in public address.

5/8/18. **San Antonio, Tex.—Conrad Kroschenski,** 20 years for alleged seditious remarks.

5/9/18. **Minneapolis, Minn.—P. L. Bernhard,** guilty of charge of hindering enlistments by telling a registrant to throw his questionnaire in the stove.

5/13/18. **Red Wing, Minn.—Joseph Gilbert,** secretary Non-Partisan League, 1 year and $500 for alleged disloyal utterances in a speech made in August, 1917.

5/15/18. **Billings, Mont.—Herman Bausch,** convicted of alleged seditious remarks.

5/15/18. **Hoboken, N. J.—Miss Margaret Davis,** 1 year for alleged seditious remarks.

5/15/18. **Bayonne, N. J.—Theo. Fedotoff** and **A. O. Taichin,** Socialists, 10 years each for alleged seditious remarks made in addressing a meeting of Russian workers for the purpose of starting a school.

5/15/18. **Los Angeles, Cal.—J. H. Shintz,** 3 months for disturbing the peace by making seditious remarks about the Liberty Loan.

5/16/18. **Los Angeles, Cal.—Mrs. G. C. Henry,** $50 or 50 days for alleged seditious utterances.

5/16/18. **Port Jervis, N. Y.—A. M. Lawson,** 3 months for alleged seditious remarks.

5/18/18. **Milwaukee, Wis.—Henry Brinkman,** 1 year for alleged seditious utterances.

5/19/18. **San Francisco, Cal.—John von Bid,** 60 days for alleged seditious utterances.

5/20/18. **Dillon, Mont.—Albert Brooks,** 7 to 15 years for

violation of state sedition act in giving away a copy of Walker C. Smith's "War and the Workers."

5/22/18. Los Angeles, Cal.—"Walking" Elliott, 90 days and $200 for alleged seditious remarks.

5/22/18. Pittsburg, Pa.—Wask Jowchalk, $50 or 60 days for alleged seditious remarks.

5/25/18. San Francisco, Cal.—Gus Schader, 30 days for alleged seditious remarks.

5/26/18. Missoula, Mont.—Herbert Mansolf, 2 to 4 years for urging a draft registrant to pay no attention to his call for physical examination.

6/—/18. Thompson Falls, Mont.—Horn, 1 year; **Weaver,** 3 months under state sedition act.

6/—/18. Kalispell, Mont.—H. Klabo, 3 months for distributing leaflets about the Tulsa outrage.

6/1/18. Martinez, Cal.—Fred Masson, 6 months for disturbing the peace by speaking disrespectfully of the Red Cross.

6/4/18. Tampa, Fla.—B. F. Burns, 90 days for alleged disloyal utterances against the President.

6/5/18. Reno, Nev.—Van Dyke, fined $100 for alleged seditious remarks.

6/13/18. Chicago, Ill.—Charles Glaser, $25 for disorderly conduct in making alleged disloyal statements.

6/13/18. Frederick, Okla.—S. K. McCord, fined $218 for alleged seditious remarks.

6/14/18. New York, N. Y.—Jacob Fabulich, 2 months for alleged seditious utterances.

6/14/18. Jersey City, N. J.—Peter Schellbach, 3 to 10 years for reviling President Wilson.

6/14/18. Jersey City, N. J.—Thomas Yarkineas, 4 to 10 years for alleged seditious remarks.

6/19/18. Minneapolis, Minn.—A. D. Smith, 1 year for the alleged remark that he "hoped the streets of Minneapolis would run a foot deep with blood."

6/23/18. Gridley, Cal.—Joseph E. Hanberg, 10 days for the alleged remark "The kaiser is the smartest man on earth, and the Germans are going to win this war, and I'm glad of it."

6/25/18. New York, N. Y.—Abraham Heller, 60 days for alleged seditious remarks.

6/29/18. San Francisco, Cal.—Artem Rudolfky, sentenced to buy $100 worth of War Saving Stamps for alleged seditious remarks concerning them.

7/16/18. San Francisco, Cal.—Waldemar Czapanski, 10 days for laughing at recruits drilling at the Presidio.

7/11/18. New York, N. Y.—John W. Rabus, 6 months for

disorderly conduct in tearing down a flag and an anti-German cartoon.

7/22/18. **Jamaica, N. Y.—Peter Grimm,** convicted for alleged seditious remarks.

7/25/18. **Middleton, N. Y.—Simon Engle,** 30 days for alleged remark that the only way the Americans would reach Berlin would be as prisoners of war.

7/31/18. **Mt. Vernon, N. Y.—Father E. W. Heinlein,** $200 and 2 months (suspended) for refusing to ring his church bells to celebrate an American victory.

7/31/18. **Los Angeles, Cal.—James A. Johnson,** a Canadian fined $300 on a charge of disturbing the peace for the alleged remark that the American soldiers in France were there only to parade its streets and salute the flag.

8/2/18. **New York, N. Y.—Frank Gerney,** 30 days for writing "Wilson, the beast of Washington" on a theatrical poster.

8/7/18. **Milwaukee, Wis.—Michael Legoth,** 3 months for alleged disparaging remarks about the U. S. government.

8/7/18. **Milwaukee, Wis.—Charles Sauer,** 9 months for alleged disparaging remarks about the U. S. government.

8/13/18. **Troy, Mont.—Tom Murphy,** fined $200 for alleged seditious remarks in violation of state sedition act.

8/24/18. **Newburgh, N. Y.—Louis Hugot,** fined $5 for disorderly conduct in making alleged seditious remarks.

9/9/18. **Pittsburgh, Pa.—Harry Bramler, George Bain, Mike Kronovitch,** each fined $25 for alleged seditious utterances.

9/20/18. **Minneapolis, Minn.—E. F. C. Ebeling,** convicted of teaching and advocating that citizens should not assist in the prosecution of the war.

9/23/18. **Norfolk, Neb.—D. M. Carr,** 10 days and $250 fine for violation of the Espionage law.

/23/18. **Norfolk, Neb.—Mack Denny,** 30 days for alleged seditious utterances.

9/23/18. **Norfolk, Neb.—Frank Hockbarth,** 4 months for violation of Espionage law.

9/26/18. **New York, N. Y.—Bernard Clark,** 6 months for alleged seditious remarks.

10/2/18. **Roselle, N. J.—Sucszar Michaelvich,** 90 days for alleged seditious remarks about the Liberty Loan.

10/2/18. **New York, N. Y.—Samuel Nikition,** 6 months for disorderly conduct in refusing to buy Liberty bonds. New trial ordered.

10/22/18. **Arlington, N. J.—Hugo Steidel,** 3 months for alleged seditious utterances.

10/24/18. **New York, N. Y.—Max Stenz and Simeon Irmont,** each 6 months for alleged seditious utterances.

10/25/18. **New York, N. Y.—Fred Cammer,** 90 days for spitting on the sidewalk near some Italian officers.

11/—/18. **Brawley, Cal.—James Ross,** 90 days and $300 fine for disturbing the peace after being tarred, feathered and beaten for alleged disloyalty.

11/19/18. **Bridgeport, Conn.—Felix Brutchase,** fined $100 and costs for alleged seditious utterances.

12/4/18. **Milwaukee, Wis.—John Corliss,** fined $200 for alleged seditious remarks.

12/6/18. **New Brunswick, N. J.—Aaron L. Gray,** fined $2,000 for alleged seditious remarks.

12/7/18. **Syracuse, N. Y.—Wm. J. Swinbourne,** 4 months for alleged seditious remarks.

1/6/19. **Seattle, Wash.—Geo. Pitkin and Louis Maki,** 30 days or $20 for distributing a circular entitled "Men of the Army Farewell."

4. PROSECUTIONS SPECIFICALLY INVOLVING I. W. W. ACTIVITY.

a). Conspiracies to violate various federal statutes.

8/30/18. **Chicago, Ill.—W. D. Haywood, Geo. Andreytchine, Ralph H. Chaplin, Aurelio V. Azuara, Richard Brazier, W. T. Nef, James Rowan, Manuel Rey, Forrest Edwards, Carl Ahlteen, Leo Laukki, C. L. Lambert, Vladimir Lossieff, Chas. Rothfisher, Sam Scarlett and Ray S. Fanning,** sentenced to twenty years; **C. W. Davis, C. H. Rice, A. B. Prashner, Fred Jakkola, Ragnar Johanson, G. J. Bourg, Stanley J. Clark, E. F. Doree, Jack Law, J. A. McDonald, J. H. Beyer, John Martin, John I. Turner, Jos. J. Gordon, Chas. Ashleigh, Dan Buckley, Alex Cournos, Ben Fletcher, Bert Lorton, Francis Miller, G. H. Perry, V. St. John, John Walsh, A. Sinclair, Peter Green, James Slovik, Chas. Bennett, Don Sheridan, J. P. Thompson, John Pancner, Sig. Stenberg, Ed. Hamilton, J. Baldazzi,** sentenced to ten years; **Wm. Moran, Dave Ingar, H. F. Kane, Wm. Weyh, P. C. Wetter, Jos. A. Oates, John Avilla, Arthur Boose, Frank Westerlund, Harry Lloyd, Joe Graber, Joe McCarty, Wm. Tanner, C. H. McKinnon, J. H. Manning, J. T. Doran, Harrison George, Peter McEvoy, Olin B. Anderson, Ted Fraser, Louis Parenti, M. Levine, Herb. McCosham, C. R. Griffin, V. V. O'Hair, James Phillips, W. H. Lewis, John M. Foss, Chas. Plahn, James Elliott** sentenced to five years; **Fred Nelson, Walter Smith, Roy A. Brown, Ray Corder, Chas. Jacobsen, A. E. Soper, Geo. Hardy, Geo. Speed, R. J. Bobba, Chas. McWhirt, J. R. Baskett, Chas. Jacobs** sentenced to one year; **Meyer Friedkin and Glen Roberts** sentenced to ten days for conspiracy to violate various sections of the Federal

Penal Code, the Espionage Act and a long list of Federal statutes.

9/31/18. **Omaha, Neb.—C. E. Bates, Roy Recker, Edward F. Dicks, John D. Ford, Joe Garner, Simon Hendrickson, Thomas A. Jenkins, Carl Jacobs, Artell Lancaster, Walter Pasewalk, Oscar Swanson, C. L. Smith, Jim Ward, George Adams, Henry Harris, Edward Hibbard, E. W. Latchem, Pat Monahan, John Nielson, John Parson, Tom Ross, Joe Ruby, Robert Weir, George Winski, Walter Wolski, Joseph J. Ratti, William Wiertola** indicted on four counts charging conspiracy under Section 37 of the Federal Penal Code. (These men were held in jail for almost a year before an indictment was found against them.)

9/24/18. **Spokane, Wash.—W. E. Hall, Joseph Kennedy, John Jockson, A. S. Embree, Guy Chesley (alias J. D. King), Jim Murphy, John Grady, Bernard Murray, Robert Scott, M. J. Smith, E. Hofstede, Jacob Franzen, Jack Sihto, Wm. D. McKenzie, W. H. Lipscomb, Sam Williams, Frank Kramer, J. S. Johnson, Matt Mathson, Robert Lassi, E. L. Olsen, Charlie Olsen, Joe Smith, John Jones, Pat McQuillin, Alex Dubay, Frank Spealman, John Westphal,** indicted on two counts charging conspiracy to violate the Espionage Act.

9/24/18. **Wichita, Kan.—C. W. Anderson, Albert Barr, A. M. Blumberg, E. M. Boyd, John Caffrey, Jim Davis, Harry Drew, Phineas Eastman, Sam Forbes, Wencil Francik, F. J. Gallagher (alias John Shannon), O. E. Gordon, James Gossard, Fred Grau, J. Gresback, Morris Hecht (alias Murrie Hecht), Ernst Henning, S. B. Hicok, Peter J. Higgins, E. J. Huber, R. A. Lambert (alias R. E. Lambert), V. W. Lyons, Paul Maihak, Harry McCarl, Tom O'Day, Frank Patton, Robert Poe, J. Pujol, Mike Quinn, J. F. Ryan, Michael Sapper, Carl Schnell, Stephen Shuren, Leo Stark, John Wallberg, George Wenger, John Woelfle, George R. Yarlott,** indicted for conspiracy to violate various Federal statutes including the Espionage Act.

1/17/19. **Sacramento, Cal.—Mortimer Downing, Frederick Esmond, Chris Luber, Phil McLaughlin, John Grave, Louis Tori, James Quinlan, Edward Quigley, George O'Connell, Roy P. Connor, John Potthast, Henry Hammer, Pete de Bernardi, Myron Sprague, Elmer Anderson, Caeser Tabib, Robert Connellan, Frank Elliott, Harry Gray, Gabe Brewer, Godfrey Ebel, William Hood, Vincent Santelli, Geo. F. Voetter,** sentenced to ten years; **Edward S. Carey, Harry Murphy, Herbert Stredwick** sentenced to five years; **Robt. Feehan, James H. Mulrooney, James Price** sentenced to four years; **Joe Carroll, Otto Elsner** sentenced to three years; **Frank Moran, Frank Reilly, Edward Anderson, Felix Cedino,** sentenced to two years; **H. Donovan, W. H. Faust, Chas. Koenig, W. L. Miller, Albert Whitehead,** sentenced to one year; **Theodora Pollok, A. L. Fox, Basil Saffores,** convicted, not yet sentenced; for alleged conspiracy to violate several sections of the Federal Penal Code, the Espionage Act and various other Federal statutes.

b. Convictions for criminal syndicalism or similar charges.

St. Maries, Ida.—E. L. Montgomery, 1 to 10 years on a charge of criminal syndicalism.

Wallace, Ida.—Joe Murphy, 1 year on a charge of criminal anarchy.

Libbey, Mont.—Geo. Strom and two others, 2 to 10 years. Nature of charge unknown.

12/—/17. **Wallace, Ida.—J. J. McMurphy,** 1 year and $500 fine for charge of criminal syndicalism.

3/—/18. **St. Maries, Ida.—W. N. Nelson,** 2 to 10 years on a charge of criminal syndicalism.

4/10/18. **Spokane, Wash.—John Brodahl, Oliver Dailey, Svan Erickson, Dennis Kelliher, Alfred Martin, Tom Salv, Robert Regan, Ira Young, Dan Paul, Tom Davis, L. M. Jones, Victor Lang, Amos Enright, Mike Diska, John Collins, Fred Johnson,** sentenced to thirty days and costs; **J. W. Johnson, J. Kelley, Pete Martin, Ed Shannon, W. T. Ward, Wm. Ray, Chas. Miama, A. Pahjola, Matt Lukla, Dorcas Lloyd** sentenced to thirty days, $100 fine and costs on a charge of vagrancy.

4/11/18. **Moscow, Ida.—T. E. Hawkins,** 6 months to 10 years, **Chas. Clifford,** 1 to 10 years, **H. E. Herd,** 4 to 10 years, on charges of criminal syndicalism.

4/15/18. **St. Maries, Ida.—Wm. Gavin,** 2 months and $100 fine for refusing to disperse when ordered to do so by the sheriff.

6/4/18. **St. Maries, Ida.—Chas. L. Anderson, Bert Banker, Frank Fleury, Henry Farner, Lyman Moore, Joe Martin, Dennis McCarthy, Fred Morgan, John Shea, J. L. O'Brien, Geo. Kopp, Robert Wilson, Charles Carlson,** 1 to 10 years for criminal syndicalism.

6/4/18. **Spokane, Wash.—Haynes Jones,** 30 days and fine of $100 and costs for violation of city criminal syndicalism ordinance.

6/11/18. **Spokane, Wash.—E. Hofstede, John Westphal, Roy McCleod, E. E. MacDonald, Adolph Guldahl,** 30 days and fine of $100 and costs for violation of city criminal syndicalism ordinance.

6/11/18. **Spokane, Wash.—John Grady,** 30 days and fine of $100 and costs for violation of city criminal syndicalism ordinance. Later held on Federal charge, now out on bail.

8/6/18. **St. John, Wash.—Lawrence Gross,** 30 days under state vagrancy law.

8/15/18. **Spokane, Wash.—Leonard Broman,** 30 days; **Ernest Rantio,** $10 fine; **Nestor Normi,** 30 days; **Gus Lind,** 30 days and $100 fine for vagrancy. All sentences suspended upon the promise of the defendants to leave town by August 17th.

III. INTERFERENCE BY PUBLIC OFFICIALS WITH RIGHT OF PEACEFUL ASSEMBLAGE.

b. General Cases

6/14/17. **Chicago, Ill.**—Public meeting of **"League of Humanity"** raided by federal officers. Four arrests were made.

8/21/17. **Hanover, Minn.—Sheriff of Hennepin Co.,** with deputies went to Hanover, Wright Co., and broke up meeting called to form a **People's Council** local.

9/16/17. **Hartford, Conn.—A. E. Whitehead and Annie R. Hale,** arrested while speaking at People's Council meeting.

9/16/17. **Minneapolis, Minn.—People's Council** forbidden by Governor to hold convention.

In November, **Scott Nearing** meetings interfered with at **Duluth, Minn., San Francisco and San Jose, Cal.**

11/12/17. **Omaha, Neb.—Construction Workers** convention of I. W. W. raided, hall wrecked and 65 members arrested.

12/8/18. **Parkston, S. D.—Socialist Party State** Convention broken up by police.

3/2/18. **Buffalo, N. Y.—Socialist Party meeting, Mrs. Kate Richard O'Hare** speaking, forbidden by City Council.

4/5/18. **New York, N. Y.—**Police close hall where **Scott Nearing** intended to speak under auspices of the Socialist Party.

5/2/18. **Niagara Falls, N. Y.—Russian Socialist** meeting broken up by chief of police because speakers talked in Russian.

b. Non-Partisan League Cases

10/4/17. **Lake City, Minn.—**Mayor and sheriff forbade meeting and brought out fire hose to disperse farmers.

10/10/17. **Mankato, Minn.—**Mayor and chairman of public safety prevented meeting.

10/12/17. **Murray Co., Minn.—**Sheriff unlawfully forbade meeting.

10/20/17. **Fergus Falls, Minn.—**Meeting forbidden.

1/9/18. **Wells, Minn.—**Sheriff and county attorney threatened violence if meeting were held.

1/14/18. **Redwood Co., Minn.—**Sheriff prohibited meeting.

1/16/18. **Pine Island, Minn.—**Mayor and constable prevented meeting.

1/18/18. **Pipestone Co., Minn.—**Meeting prevented.

1/25/18. **Hatfield, Minn.**—Speaker arrested by sheriff and meeting broken up during a patriotic loyalty talk.

1/26/18. **Belle Plain, Minn.**—Sheriff broke up meeting.

2/7/18. **Bertha, Minn.**—Meeting in a co-operative potato warehouse broken up by deputy sheriff and mayor.

2/— 18. **Walters, Minn.**—Meeting stopped by sheriff.

IV. SEARCH AND SEIZURE.

Including only the important cases. While most of these raids were made with proper warrants, some of them were not, even when conducted by federal agents. Scores of minor raids by local officials have been conducted without lawful warrants.

1. I. W. W. Cases.

9/5/17. Every **I. W. W.** Hall in the country raided by federal officers.

11/13/17. **Miami, Ariz.**—**I. W. W.** hall and office of the Local Defense Council raided by cavalry, deputy sheriffs and agents of the Dept. of Justice. All literature and records were taken.

11/17/17. **Fresno, Cal.**—House of **Fred Little**, an I. W. W., raided for third time by Federal officers.

12/17/17. **Chicago, I..**—**I. W. W. headquarters** raided and occupied for 12 days by Federal officers. Several thousand dollars worth of literature was confiscated.

12/20/17. **Seattle, Wash.**—**I. W. W. Defense Committee** headquarters and offices of Industrial Worker raided by federal officers with search warrant who seized all records, furniture, etc.

12/21/17. **Cleveland, O.**—Plant of **International Publishing Co.** raided by agents of Department of Justice and many I. W. W. and Socialist posters seized.

1/23/18. **Spokane, Wash.**—Office of **Spokane Defense Committee of I. W. W.** raided by federal officers. **John Grady, J. W. Rittenhouse, Fred Kennedy, Tom Scott and David Jennes** arrested and all books, papers and literature seized.

2/23/18. **Portland, Ore.**—**I. W. W.** hall raided by federal officers. Fifty arrests made and all literature and records seized.

5/3/18. **Seattle, Wash.**—**I. W. W.** hall raided by police. Two hundred and thirteen arrests made and much literature seized.

9/24/18. **Tacoma, Wash.**—**I. W. W.** hall raided, literature and records seized and 33 men arrested.

1918—**San Francisco, Cal.**—Headquarters of **California Defense Committee** raided seven times while preparing for Sacramento trial. Secretary arrested as a "vagrant" fifteen times within the year.

2. International Bible Students' Association

3/1/18. **Brooklyn, N. Y.**—Two auto loads of literature seized by Military Intelligence Bureau.

3/3/18. **Los Angeles, Cal**—Three thousand copies of **"The Finished Mystery"** seized by the Military Intelligence Bureau.

3/5/18. **Hazelton, Pa.**—Headquarters **I. B. S. A.** raided and 200 books confiscated by American Protective League agents.

3/14/18. **Omaha, Neb.**—4,000 copies of **"The Finished Mystery"** seized on Federal warrant.

3/16/18. **Fort Washington, Texas.**—5,000 copies **"The Finished Mystery"** seized by federal officials.

3/17/18. **St. Louis, Mo.**—10,000 copies **"The Finished Mystery"** seized by agents of Dept. of Justice.

3/23/18. **Lisbon, O.**—Fifteen copies of **"The Finished Mystery"** seized by Sheriff on orders from federal authorities.

3/24/18. **Galveston, Texas.**—45,000 copies of **"The Finished Mystery"** seized by Federal deputy marshal.

4/29/18. **Los Angeles, Cal.**—Headquarters of **I. B. S. A.** raided by federal authorities. Two arrests made and all books and records seized.

3. Other Cases

8/28/17. **Philadelphia, Pa.**—Headquarters, Socialist party, raided by federal authorities. Three arrests made and papers seized.

9/5/17. **Chicago, Ill.**—Offices of National Socialist Party raided by Federal officers.

9/6/17. **Chicago, Ill.**—Officers of four Socialist newspapers, **Arbeiter Zeitung, Socialist Demokraten, Radnicka-Straza, The Radical Press** raided by the Federal officers with search warrants. Much literature and plates were seized.

9/13/17. **Toledo, O.**—**Scott Nearing's** house raided by Federal officers.

9/14/17. **Dertoit, Mich.**—Offices of Socialist Labor Party raided by Federal authorities. Books and literature seized.

9/29/17. **Columbus, O.**—Social Labor Party offices raided.

10/5/17. **Cincinnati, O.**—People's Church raided by local U. S. attorney. Papers seized and held for over a year.

12/21/17. **Palo, Alto, Cal.**—Houses of **J. F. Pilz, J. Mills, Vincent J. Neilson, Mrs. M. S. Alderton** raided by federal officers, some literature seized.

12/29/17. **San Francisco, Cal.**—House of **Alexander and Louise Harding Horr** raided while owners were in jail in default of excessive bail exacted after their arrest on charge of "not moving on."

1/23/18. **Los Angeles, Cal.**—**Nobert Myles**, held for 5 days without warrant by military authorities.

1/23/18. **Cleveland, O.**—Socialist Party offices raided by Federal officers.

3/27/18. **San Francisco, Cal.—People's Council** office raided by officials several times.

4/22/18. **Lorain, O.**—Protective League and federal agents raided a Socialist meeting arresting 16 and seizing many books.

4/22/18. **Connellsville, Pa.**—Home of **Wm. and Christy Hang** raided by town constable. A printing press and pamphlets entitled "The Devil's Rake-off" and "Don't Blame the War on the Devil" were found.

4/26/18. **Pittsburgh, Pa.**—Literature including 26 copies of **Rev. W. A. Prosser's** book "Militarism" seized by agents of the Department of Justice.

2/30/18. **Seattle, Wash.**—State headquarters of the **Socialist Party** raided, over 700 pieces of literature seized by federal authorities.

5/5/18. **Lorain, O.**—W.I.I.U. hall raided by federal agents. Twenty arrests made and a truck load of literature and records seized.

5/8/18. **Brooklyn, N. Y.**—Home of **Stephen Binder** raided by federal agents. Binder was arrested and several hundred copies of an alleged seditious book entitled "Light and Truth" written by him were seized.

5/21/18. **Batavia, Ill.**—Home of **Mrs. John Anderson** raided by federal agents, 400 copies of alleged seditious book entitled "Reduced Privilege Class Education" by Dr. W. C. Langhorst.

5/22/18. **Pittsburgh, Pa.**—Socialist Party headquarters raided by police, files and literature removed, sixteen arrests.

8/27/18. **Spokane, Wash.**—Office of **Miss Clara M. Irvin** raided by federal authorities. Letter by E. Hofstede seized among other things.

8/30/18. **New York, N. Y.**—Office of **N. Y. Bureau of Legal Advice** raided by officials of Department of Justice. Raid based upon an invalid search warrant.

8/31/18. **New York, N. Y.**—Offices of **National Civil Liberties Bureau and of Walter Nelles,** its counsel, raided by officials of Department of Justice. Raid based upon invalid search warrants.

9/13/18. **Portland, Oregon.**—Room of **Mrs. Alice Park** at Hotel Lenox searched by federal officers. Much material seized without warrant.

11/8/18. **Chicago, Ill.**—Home and office of **Theo. Lunde** raided by Federal authorities and much literature seized.

12/31/18. **Philadelphia, Pa.**—City detectives and postal inspectors raided **Socialist headquarters and bookstore.**

1/16/19. **Niagara Falls, N. Y.**—Apartment of **Jos. Spivak,** secretary of League for Amnesty of Political Prisoners raided by federal authorities.

V. Conscientious Objectors in Prison, March 1, 1919

The following list of 179 conscientious objectors so far as the Bureau has been able to ascertain were still confined in Federal Prisons, civil or military, on March 1, 1919. Almost all of them are in the Disciplinary Barracks at Fort Leavenworth, Kansas. It is probable that the following list does not include more than half the conscientious objectors still in confinement at that date.

1 YEAR
Bieber, Abraham

3 YEARS
Huckelberry, Earl
Muhlke, Fred. J.
Robinette, Eddie
Wittrock, Gus.

4 YEARS
Siro, Verner

5 YEARS
Larson, Eno R.

6 YEARS
Simons, H. Austin

10 YEARS
Blair, N. J.
Clayton, Elias
Dart, Vane V.
Falk, Morris
Franke, Robt. W., Jr.
Haga, John
Harkey, Stephen
Heath, Edward J.
Hershberger, Samuel M.
Kantor, Wm.
Krjworuk, Wassili
Levering, John
Maher, Walfred E.
Martin, Henry D.
Moser, Frank
Penick, Fred

Reed, Thomas
Salty, Gustav
Thomas, Mark R.
Wells, Ernest P.
Whitaker, Earl
Yanyar, Adolph L.

12 YEARS
Haessler, Carl

15 YEARS
Allinson, Brent D.
Arbitman, Samuel
Blumenthal, Louis H.
Brenneman, J. L.
Bruber, Harold
Buck, Frank, Jr.
Buzzi, Alfred
Clave, Harry
Daisenberger, Ward C.
DeCessa, Gerald
Edwards, Thomas Todd
Fullwood, Albert
Grunzig, Bruno
Hirshberg, Walter L.
Horlacher, Roy
Humphries,—
LaCasale, Nicola
Marcowitz, Lazarus B.
Mohr, Charles E.
Ostrom, Eric
Powell, Rexford
Prince, Andrew Gust.

Quinn, Joseph H.
Robinson, Karl
Sandin, Max
Schmidt, John
Schnieder, H.
Smith, Louis
Smith, Aaron
Stanley, Stephen
Stepanovitch, Fritz
Walter, J. M.
Wangerin, Otto
Weiershauser, Geo.
Wenger, Rolla S.
Wheeler, Chas E.
Wheeler, Oscar O.
White, Joe
Wood, Russell R.
Wurz, J. M.

20 YEARS
Alexander, Americo
Broms, A. S.
Clodi, Chas.
Dunn, John T.
Eichel, Julius
Grass, John
Hiller, Theodore
Iverson, I. M.
James, W. Oral
Leighton, Fred'k W.
Maki, Sander
Morgan, Thomas
Mullis, Frank
Petroshki, Tony
Rasmussen, P.
Sorenson, L.
Wortsmann, Jacob
Wortsmann, Gustav

25 YEARS
Cage, H. S.
Carlson, Axel W.
Carlson, R. A.
Davis, Guy
Edwards, Wm. H.
Franklin, Morris
Gergotz, L. J.
Johnson, Carl W.

Johnson, Gunnard
Kamman, Morris
Kas, John
Lunde, Erling
Magruder, H. Stanley
Robinson, Fred A.
Treseler, W. H.
Ungar, Nickolaus
Wilson, Arthur

30 YEARS
Doty, —
Grossner, Philip B.
Sterenstein, Samuel
Wagner, David

35 YEARS
Rose, Jacob W.

SENTENCE UNKNOWN
Bach, Isidor
Beck, Hans
Bernstein, Meyer
Bloch, Hyman
Bloch, Morris
Breger, Benj.
Briedert, William
Briehl, Fred
Calvi, —
Caplowitz, Phillip
Clay, Charles T.
Crofton, Julian
Danielwicz, Leo
Demsey, Roy
Danbrowsky, Julius
Duncan, Martin S.
Eichel, David
Fast, —
Fernquist, Gustaf
Fox, Robert
Greenberg, Julius
Getts, Clark
Heckman, Adin E.
Hennessy, Francis X.
Hess, Maurice A.
Hofer, David
Hofer, Michael (died in prison)
Hofer, — (died in prison)
Jasmagy, William

Jerger, Fred
Kaplan, Hyman
Kitterman, —
Kleinsouser, Sam
Kchnowicz, —
Kleinsouser, Paul
Kulikoff, John
Laub, E. F. C.
Lee, Harry
Livingston, James V.
Logan, Wallace F.
Marshall, Stanley
Mauer, —
McPherson, Chas. E.
Metzler, Ray
Miller, Payson
Monsky, Henry
Moore, Howard
Moran, —

Murch, James A
Meyers, J. C.
Neuenschwander, Abr.
Oelco, Isidore
Platin, Eric R.
Poplovitch, —
Proctor, Will D.
Rodolph, Charles Carleton
Salmon, Benj. J.
Sandberg, Wm.
Seidenberg, Roderick
Shuben, Andrew
Silver, Emmanuel
Steiner, —
Strangland, —
Susoff, Ivan
Uren, Fred
Waters, —
Wipf, Jacob
Wingert, —

VI. Miscellaneous Cases of Dismissal from Public or Academic Service for Alleged Anti-War Views or Activities.

New York.—**Benjamin Glassberg, Samuel Schmalhausen, Thomas Mufson, A. Henry Schneer, Gertrude Pignol,** high school teachers, dismissed at various time for alleged disloyalty.

7/—/17. **St. Paul, Minn.**—**Frank A. Webster,** post office employe, discharged for furnishing bail for three men who did not register.

8/10/17. **Marion, Ohio.**—**M. L. Martin,** mail carrier, dismissed for being on the reception committee for an anti-draft speaker.

10/—/17. **New York.**—**J. McKeen Cattell** and **H. W. L. Dana** dismissed from Columbia University for comments upon governmental policies in relation to the war.

11/3/17. **Bronville, Ind.**—**F. S. Lamonte,** Socialist attorney, disbarred for alleged disloyal speeches.

11/25/17. **Charlottesville, Va.**—The appointment of **Prof. Leonidas Whipple** rescinded because of alleged seditious remarks made in a speech at Sweetbrier College.

12/17/17. **Los Angeles, Cal.**—**Rev. L. P. Ryland** removed as superintendent of Los Angeles district of the Southern California Conference of the M. E. Church for alleged pacifist ideas.

12/11/17. **Carson City, Nevada.**—**Miss Dorothy Adams,** school teacher, dismissed for alleged disloyal utterances.

12/27/17. **Indianapolis, Ind.**—**Chas. W. Baumann,** patrolman, discharged for alleged disloyal remarks.

12/31/17. **Indianapolis, Ind.**—**Chas. Best,** 73 years of age, discharged by Columbia Harness Co. for alleged disloyal remarks.

2/11/18. **New Ulm, Minn.**—Resignation of **Pres. Adolph Ackerman** demanded by the trustees for alleged anti-draft activities.

2/13/18. **Denver, Colo.**—**Ellen Kennan** and **Gertrude Nafe,** school teachers, dismissed for striking the word "obedience" from a "loyalty pledge."

3/5/18. **Omaha, Nebraska.—Miss Esther Larson** dropped for refusal to salute the flag for religious reasons.

2/14/18. **Harrisburg, Pa.—Prof. H. C. Liebig,** dismissed from high school faculty for alleged pro-Germanism.

3/9/18. **Bangor, Me.—Wm. E. Walz,** dean of the law school of the University of Maine, dismissed for alleged pro-Germanism.

3/12/18. **New York, N. Y.—Miss Mary McDowell,** a Quaker, suspended from her position at the Manual Training High School for her views against war.

/13/18. **Ann Arbor, Mich.—W. W. Florer, John Dieterle, W. W. Kostermann, Herman Wiegand and Richard Ficken** dropped for alleged pro-Germanism.

5/1/18. **Berkeley, Cal.—George W. Han,** a reader in the University of California, dismissed for "disloyal and seditious" utterances.

5/11/18. **Portland, Ore.—I. Kimmons,** draughtsman in county assessor's office dismissed because he was opposed to war on religious grounds.

5/13/18. **Newark, N. J.—Fred Wusterbarth's** citizenship revoked for alleged pro-German utterances.

5/24/18. **Los Angeles, Cal.—Mary Brueger,** daughter of a civil war veteran, dismissed from her position as teacher because she was the wife of an unnaturalized German.

6/8/18. **Washington, D. C.—Cleveland Abbe, Jr.,** dismissed from weather bureau for his "well-known sympathies for the Imperial German Government."

6/12/18. **Columbus, O.—Fred Albrink,** inspector for state highway commission suspended after being found guilty of disloyalty at a hearing held by the League of American Patriots.

6/17/18. **Olympia, Wash.—C. R. Carr,** school teacher dismissed for alleged disloyalty.

6/19/18. **Lincoln, Neb.**—The resignation of **Professors E. B. Hopt, E. E. Persingerand, G. W. A. Lucker** demanded by the board of regents for a lack of "American aggressiveness in their attitude toward the war."

6/26/18. **San Francisco, Cal.—Rose Levin** refused a high school diploma for saying "Though born in this city, I owe allegiance to no flag but the red flag of Socialism."

7/11/18. **San Francisco, Cal.—F. A. Varrelman,** high school teacher, dismissed for alleged disloyalty.

9/15/18. **Minneapolis, Minn.—Prof. W. A. Schaper** dismissed for "unwillingness to aid the U. S. in the war."

10/26/18. **St. Louis, Mo.**—Saloon of **Frank Hieminz** closed by excise commissioner for alleged disloyal utterances.

12/19/18. **Rochester, Minn.—George P. Criseler,** high school teacher, removed for advocating public ownership in a private conversation.

ADDENDA.

Since going to press the President upon the recommendation of the Attorney-General, has issued pardons and commutations of sentences with respect to the cases of fifty-three persons convicted under the Espionage Act. The list is as follows; the sentence in each case being as commuted:

G. C. Carter, a year and a day.
Henry A. Kellar, sentence to expire 4/1/19.
Charles Sahrbacher, sentence to expire 4/1/19.
Sydney Mader, sentence to expire 4/1/19.
M. P. Fogh, sentence to expire 9/1/19.
W. H. Rockey, one year.
R. E. Doris, eighteen months.
Harold G. Mackley, three years.
W. A. Easman, sentence to expire 4/1/19.
Joseph E. Hamburg, sentence to expire 4/1/19.
Ernest Meier, $250 fine.
John Moes, sentence to expire 4/1/19.
F. M. Romero, sentence to expire 4/1/19.
Gustave Sigwalt, sentence to expire 4/1/19.
Fritz Bisdorf, two years.
Anton Bayer, sentence to expire 4/1/19.
Frank Schafer, one year.
James Hanaman, sentence to expire 7/1/19.
R. F. Lahnemann, sentence to expire 4/1/19.
Dan Hamilton, sentence to expire 4/1/19.
Gustave H. Taubert, eighteen months .
J. A. Miller, one year.
Anthony Frederick, one year.
Otto Janson, two years.
L. H. Sturm, one year.
Everitt G. Engelin, two years.
Emil Keifer, sentence to expire 4/1/19.
Carl de Schell, a year and a day.
Daniel Mahoney, a year and a day.
J. J. Conley, one year.
F. C. Blumlein, sentence to expire 4/1/19.
John Liebig, one year.

Paul Bosco, two years.
Arnie von Harder, three years.
George H. Hogan, a year and a day.
William Bago, one year.
Christian S. Schunke, one year.
L. N. LeGendre, sentence to expire 4/1/19.
Arthur Roth, one year.
Martin Johnson, sentence to expire 4/1/19.
Charles Bernal, two years.
C. M. Nelson, a year and a day.
John O'Connell, two years.
C. P. Menke, sentence to expire 4/1/19.
John Meyers, one year.
Chris Ammer, two years.
Frederick Krafft, full pardon.
Robert Goldstein, three years.
Silas Saylor, a year and a day.
Theodore Buessel, sentence to expire 4/1/19.
Flora I. Foreman, two years.
Clarence H. Waldron, sentence to expire 4/1/19
Amos L. Hitchcock, two years.

INDEX

Abbe, Cleveland, Jr. 95	Baldwin, R. N. ---- 27	Bold, S. ------------ 29
Abrahms, Jacob---- 22	Barnes, C. W. ------ 12	Bollman, F. K. ----- 11
Abrahamson, Louis- 29	Barr, A. ----------- 35	Bontrager, M. C. -- 20
Ackerman, A.------- 44	Barrett, W. -------- 23	Boose, A. ---------- 34
Adams, Miss D.----- 44	Baskett, J. R. ----- 34	Barer, E. ---------- 21
Adams, Geo.-------- 35	Bates, C. E. ------- 35	Bosco, P. -------14,18
Ahlteen, Carl------- 34	Bates, Wm. -------- 10	Bosses, Y. --------- 15
Albers, Henry ----- 18	Battigo, L. -------- 6	Bostrom, F. -------- 25
Albrink, Fred------- 45	Baumann, Ch. W. -- 44	Bourg, G. J. -------- 11
Alderton, M. S. ---- 39	Bausch, H. -------- 31	Boutill, I. T. ------- 21
Alexander, A. ---- 42	Bayer, A. ---------- 47	Boyd, E. M. -------- 35
Allenbach, Geo ---- 8	Beard, W. P. ------ 19	Brackett, Wm. A. -- 18
Allinson, B. D. ---- 41	Beayans, J. -------- 25	Bramler, H. -------- 33
Am. Fed. of L. ---- 9	Beck, H. ---------- 42	Brazier, R. --------- 34
Am. Socialist Soc. -- 22	Beck, J. M. -------- 28	Breidel, Geo. ------- 13
Ameringer, O. ---- 24	Becker, L. --------- 10	Breger, B. --------- 42
Ammer, Chris. ----- 48	Becker, M. --------- 27	Brenneman, J. L. -- 41
Anbelsen, H. ------ 30	Beckstrom, J. W. -- 30	Brewer, G. D. ------ 30
Anderson, Chas. L.- 36	Beilfuss, P. -------- 6	Brewer, G. --------- 35
Anderson, C. W. -- 35	Benecke, A. M. ---- 27	Bruher, H. --------- 41
Anderson, Edw. ---- 35	Bennett, Ch. ------- 34	Briedert, W. ------- 42
Anderson, E. ------ 35	Bentall, J. O. ------ 19	Briehl, F. ---------- 42
Anderson, Mrs. J. -- 40	Benzin, A. F. W. --- 17	Brinkman, H. ------ 31
Anderson, Olin B. - 34	Benthal, J. O. ----- 26	Brodahl, J. -------- 36
Anding, Chas. ---- 16	Bergen, F. Mrs. ---- 6	Broman, L. --------- 37
Andreytchine, Geo. 34	Berger, V. ------ 20, 24	Broms, A. S. ---- 28, 42
Anton, Adolph ---- 7	Berkman, A. ------- 27	Brooks, A. --------- 31
Arbitman, S. ------ 41	Bernal, Ch. -------- 48	Brooks, E. K. ------- 25
Armbruster, J. ---- 14	Benardy, P. -------- 35	Brondau, S. M. ---- 23
Armburgh, Wm. E. 20	Bernhard, P. L. ---- 31	Brown, Roy A. ---- 34
Arnold, L. --------- 24	Bernstein, M. ------ 42	Brueger, M. ------- 45
Aranson, P. ------- 12	Best, Ch. ---------- 44	Boutchase F. ------- 34
Ashleigh, Chas. ---- 34	Beyer, J. H. -------- 34	Buch, F., Jr. ------- 41
Auerswald, Rev. C. 19	Bias, H. ----------- 27	Buckley, Dan ------ 34
Aurin, H. ---------- 27	Bid, J. ------------- 31	Buessel, T. --------- 48
Avella, J. ---------- 34	Bieber, A. --------- 41	Bunyard, C. -------- 18
Axelroad, I. ------- 29	Bienneman, J. C. -- 7	Busch, F. J. -------- 28
Azuara, A. V. ----- 34	Bigelow, H. S. ----- 5	Buzzi, A. ---------- 41
Bach, I. ----------- 42	Binder, S. --------- 22	Cabet, A. ---------- 28
Bago, W. -------- 16, 48	Birkner, J. M. ------ 7	Caffry, Yuo -------- 35
Bain, G. ----------- 33	Bisdorf, F. ------17, 47	Cage, H. S. --------- 42
Baker, C. ---------- 26	Blair, N. J. -------- 41	Callen, W. W. ------ 13
Baker, Fred. ------- 29	Bloch, H. ---------- 42	Calvi, ------------- 42
Baker, R. E. ------- 24	Bloch, M. ---------- 42	Canter, A. M. ------ 6
Balcom, Dr. F. O. -- 18	Blodgett, D. T. ---- 21	Capers, H. C. ------ 7
Baldazzi, J. -------- 34	Blumberg, A. M. -- 35	Caplowitz, Ph. ---- 42
Ballam, J. J. ------- 19	Blumenthal, L. H. -- 41	Capo, V. B. -------- 19
Baltzer, E. -------- 21	Blumlein, F. C. ---- 47	Carey, E. S. -------- 35
Von Bauls, H. ----- 14	Bobba, R. J. ------- 34	Carlisle, Geo. ------ 10
Banker, B. --------- 36	Boehner, L. W. ---- 18	Carlson, A. W. ---- 42

Carlson, Ch. 36	De Cessa, G. 41	Embree, A. S. 35
Carlson, R. A. 42	Defense Committee 38	Enders, Ed. 24
Carr, C. R. 45	Dell, F. 25	Engelin, E. G. 47
Carr, D. M. 33	Demsey, R. 42	Engels, Ch. 24
Carrol, J. 35	Denny, M. 18, 33	Engle, S. 33
Carter, C. C. 47	Denson, Wm. A. 25	Enfield, O. C. 19
Casey, J. E. 14	Derman, Wm. 29	Engdahl, L. J. 20
Cattell, J. McK. 5, 44	Deutsch 27	Engelin, E. A. 19
Cattell, O. 26	Deutscher H. 7	Enright, A. 36
Cecca, G. de 20	Dicks, E. F. 35	Equi, Dr. M. 20
Cedino, F. 35	Dickson, C. 17	Erdtmann, G. 16
Chaplin, R. H. 34	Dieterle, J. 45	Erickson, S. 36
Chesley, G. 35	Diska, M. 36	Ervick, P. 30
Cheyney, C. R. 26	Dodge, Wm. 20	Eschman, L. J. 8
Chovenson, S. H. 9	Dae, P. 21	Esmond, F. 35
Christian Pacifists 5	Doeppling, A. Rev. 31	Esser, F. 31
Church of the L. G. 8	Donoran, H. 35	Evanicki, L. 18
Clark, B. 33	Doran, J. T. 34	Fabulich, J. 32
Clark, S. J. 34	Doree, E. F. 34	Fadel, H. 27
Clave, H. 41	Doris, R. E. 47	Fairchild, F. 22
Clay, Ch. T. 42	Doty 42	Falk, M. 41
Clayton, E. 41	Douglas, J. 16	Fanning, R. F. 34
Clodi, Ch. 42	Downing, M. 35	Farmer, H. 36
Coats, T. C. 24	Drenks, Ch. 10	Fast, 42
Coldwell, J. M. 20	Drew, H. 35	Faust, W. H. 35
Collins, J. 36	Duboy, A. 35	Fay, H. A. 11
Colins, Rev. M. D. 23	Dudas, L. 11	Fay, H. A. 11
Connellan, Rbt. 35	Duncan, M. S. 42	Feodotoff, T. 31
Connor, R. P. 35	Duncan, W. B. 9	Feehan, R. 35
Construction W'k's 37	Dunn, J. T. 42	Feifer, E. 47
Cook, D. 10	Dunning, J. 28	Feiron, A. 17
Co-operative Stores 13	Dunton, M. 16	Feldman, F. A. 18
Cooperider, W. 8	Dutsch, H. 5	Feltman, H. 17, 23
Corder, R. 34	Duxbury, H. 10	Felton, M. 23
Corliss, J. 34	Dyke, V. 32	Ferlan, J. 30
Cornell, T. 19	Easman, W. A. 47	Fernquist, G. 42
Cournos, A. 34	Eastman, M. 25	Ficken, R. 45
Crammer, F. 34	Eastman, P. 35	Finnish I. W. W. 12
Criseler, G. P. 46	Ebbits, W. A. 29	Finished Mystery 39
Crofton, J. 42	Ebel, G. 35	Firth, E. 27
Cully, J. 26	Ebeleng, E. F. C. 33	Fisher, G. H. 20
Czapanski, W. 32	Edwards, F. 34	Fletcher, B. 34
Dana, H. W. L. 5, 44	Edwards, T. T. 41	Fleury, F. 36
Danbrowsky, J. 42	Edwards, Wm. H. 42	Florer, W. H. 45
Danielwicz, L. 42	Edwards, W. R. 13	Fogh, M. P. 47
Davis, C. H. 34	Ehrhard, Wm. 16	Forbes, S. 35
Davis, G. 42	Eichel, D. 42	Ford, E. 28
Davis, J. 35	Eichel, J. 42	Ford, E. B. 28
Davis, Miss M. 31	Einem, Curt, Von 17	Ford, J. D. 35
Davis, T. 36	Eliason, Wm. 15	Foreman, F. Mrs. 18
Debs, E. V. 20	Elliott, "Walking" 32	Foss, J. M. 34
Daily, O. 36	Elliott, F. 35	Foster, E. 11
Daesenberger, W. C. 41	Elliott, J. 34	Foster, L. 14
Darby, F. M. 17	Ellis J. H. 5	Fox, A. L. 35
Darkow, M. 20, 25	Elmer, Wm. P. 18	Fox, R. 42
Dart, V. V. 41	Elsmer, H. 30	Frachter, J. 27
	Elsner, O. 35	Fraina, L. C. 26

Francik, W. _____ 35	Gross, L. _____ 37	Hehir, J. _____ 27
Freinke, Ch. _____ 9	Grosner, Ph. B. ____ 42	Heller, T. _____ 42
Franke, R. U., Jr. __ 41	Grunzig, B. _____ 41	Hennessy, F. X.____ 42
Franklin, M. _____ 42	Guldhal, A. _____ 36	Henning, E. _____ 35
Frantz, Y. H. _____ 16	Gustoff, R. _____ 9	Hershberger, S. M._ 41
Franzen, J. _____ 35	Gutormse, Mrs. C. __ 23	Hess, M. _____ 42
Frazer, Ted _____ 34	Haessler, C. _____ 41	Heynacher, W. _____ 15
Frazer, B. _____ 27	Haga, J. _____ 41	Hibbard, E. _____ 35
Frederick, A. _____ 47	Hale, A. R. _____ 37	Hickman, C. C. _____ 11
Free, J. V. _____ 26	Hale, M. V. _____ 9	Hicks, W. M. Rev. 7, 18
French, E. J. _____ 9	Hall, Ves _____ 24	Hicok, S. B. _____ 35
Friederich, A. _____ 6	Hall, W. E. _____ 35	Himinz, F. _____ 46
Friedkin, M. _____ 34	Hamburg, J. E. ____ 47	Higgins, P. J. _____ 35
Frohwerk, J. _____ 20	Hamilton, D. _____ 47	Hirshberg, W. L.___ 41
Fullwood, A. _____ 41	Hamilton, E. _____ 34	Hitchcock, A. L. 20, 48
Gaebler, F. _____ 23	Hamilton, R. R. ____ 12	Hoegen, M., Von___ 6
Gamss, Rev. J. ____ 26	Hammer, H. _____ 35	Hodges, Wm. _____ 14
Gallagher, F. J. ____ 35	Han, G. H. _____ 45	Hofer _____ 42
Garner, J. _____ 35	Hanaman, J. _____ 47	Hoffman, H. _____ 6
Gavin, Wm. _____ 36	Hanberg, J. E. ____ 32	Hofstede, E. _26, 35, 36
Geizler, F. _____ 14	Hang, Chr. _____ 40	Hogan, G. H._____ 48
George, H. _____ 35	Hang, Wm. _____ 40	Horlacher, R. _____ 41
Gerdes, Rev. D. ___?	Harder A. _____ 48	Holt, Jas. _____7, 10
Gerdes, J. B. _____ 26	Harden, R. _____ 14	Holzman, H. A.____ 10
Gergotz, L. J. _____ 42	Hardin, F. _____ 28	Homan, H. _____ 15
Germer, A. _____ 20, 24	Harding, E. _____ 25	Hood, Wm. _____ 35
Gerney, F. _____ 33	Hardy, Geo. _____ 34	Hopt, Prof. E. B.___ 45
Getts, C. _____ 42	Harkey, S. _____ 41	Horn _____ 32
Gilbert, J. _____ 29, 31	Harper, S. J. _____ 25	Horr, A. _____29, 39
Glaser, Ch. _____ 32	Harrington, J. ____ 31	Horr, L. H. _____ 39
Glassberg, B. _____ 44	Harris, H. _____ 35	Houston, Wm. _____ 16
Glesser, C. _____ 19	Harris, N. M. _____ 7	Howes, H. _____ 27
Glison, G. L. _____ 27	Harrison, Geo. ____ 34	Huber, E. J._____ 35
Golden, J. O. _____ 13	Hathaway, M. ____ 12	Huckelberry, E. ____ 41
Goldman, E. _____ 27	Hauer, J. _____ 31	Hugot, L. _____ 33
Goldstein, R. ____ 19, 48	Hawkins, T. E. ____ 36	Humphries _____ 41
Gordon, J. J. _____ 34	Haywood, W. D. __ 34	Hunter, Wm. A. ____ 8
Gordon, O. E. _____ 35	Head, Wm. J._____ 21	Industrial Worker _ 12
Gossard, J. _____ 35	Heath, E. J. _____ 41	Ingar, D. _____ 34
Graber, J. _____ 39	Hecht, M. _____ 35	Inter. Pub. Co. ____ 38
Grocely, E. _____ 14	Heckman, A. E. ____ 42	I. W. W. _____11, 12
Grady, J. _____ 36, 38	Heinlein, Father E.	International Bible
Grady, J. _____ 35	W. _____ 33	Students Ass'n._9, 39
Grass, J. _____ 42	Held, E. _____ 18	Irmont, S. _____ 33
Grats, Wm. _____ 7	Heller, A. _____ 32	Iverson. I. M._____ 42
Grave, J. _____ 35	Hendricksen, H. M._ 15	Irvin, Miss C. M.___ 40
Gray, A. L. _____ 34	Hendricks, Miss R.	Isensee, Wm. _____ 15
Gray, H. _____ 35	M. _____ 31	Jablowsky, A. _____ 22
Green, B. _____ 27	Hendrickson, S. ____ 35	Jacobs, C. _____ 35
Grau, F. _____ 35	Hennacy, A. A._____ 26	
Green, P. _____ 34	Hennig, Paul _____ 24	
Greenberg, J. _____ 42	Henning, J. _____ 26	
Gresback, J._____ 35	Henry, Mrs. G. C.__ 31	
Griffen, C. B. _____ 9	Herd, H. E. _____ 36	
Griffin, C. R. _____ 34	Herman, H. _____ 22	
Grimm, P. _____ 33	Heltner, Rev. _____ 23	
Groeschl, E. _____ 24	Hett, O. _____ 24	

Jacobs, S. 15	Kleinsouser, S. 43	Leitzes, M. 27
Jacobs, C. 34	Kleist, J. C. 24	Levering, J. 41
Jacobsen, C. 34	Klinge, Chas. 7	Levine, M. 34
Jager, H. 27	Klug, A. 24	Levin, Rose 45
Jakkola, F. 34	Koch, C. 11	Levine, N. 28
James, W. O. 42	Koenig, H. C. 26	Levinson, H. 27
Janson, O. 15, 47	Kopp, Geo. 36	Levitt, A. 28
Jasick, L. 25	Koenig, C. 35	Lewis, J. A. 12
Jasmagy, W. 42	Koerber, Dr. A. 23	Lewis, W. H. 34
Jenkins, T. A. 35	Koetzer, G. 9	Liebig, H. C. 45
Jennes, D. 38	Kolar, J. 16	Liebig, J. 47
Jerger, F. 43	Kolbe, E. A. 16	Liebisch, G. 15
Jesky, S. 30	Kolbe, F. 11	Lieske, August 8
Jockson, J. 35	Kornmann, C. 15, 7	Lind, Gus 37
Johanson, R. 34	Koski, E. 12	Lind, H. C. 11
Johnson, C. W. 42	Koralsgy, J. 6	Lindenberg, S. 30
Johnson, F. 36	Kostermann, W. W. 45	Lippman, S. 22
Johnson, G. 42	Kowalsky, G. 16	Lipscomb, W. H. 35
Johnson, J. S. 35	Krafft, F. 19, 48	Little, Frank 11
Johnson, J. W. 36	Kramer, F. 35	Livingston, J. V. 43
Johnson, J. A. 33	Kramer, L. 27	Lloyd, D. 36
Johnson, M. 48	Kronovitch, M. 33	Lloyd, H. 34
Jones, H. 36	Kroschenski, C. 31	Logan, W. F. 43
Jones, J. 35	Kruse, J. H. 17, 23	Logeda, M. 29
Jones, L. M. 36	Kruse, W. F. 20	Lorton, B. 34
Jones, M. M. 23	Krjworuk, W. 41	Lossieff, V. 34
Jordon, D. S. 5	Kubecka, J. 8	Luber, C. 35
Jordan, F. 29	Kulekoff, J. 43	Lucker, G. W. A. 45
Jowchalk, W. 32	Kuntson, A. 13	Lukla, M. 36
Julius, A. 10	Kunz, J. 16	Lunde, T. 40
Julius, F. 10	LaCasale, N. 41	Lundin, G. 6
Kamann, C. H. 19	Lachowsky, H. 22	Lyons, V. W. 35
Kamman, M. 42	Lahnemann, R. F. 47	McCarl, H. 35
Kane, H. F. 34	Lambert, C. L. 34	McCarthy, D. 36
Kantor, Wm. 41	Lambert, R. A. 35	McCarthy, J. 34
Kaplan, H. 43	Lamonte, F. S. 44	McCleod, R. 36
Kas, J. 42	Lancaster, A. 35	McCord, S. K. 32
Katkus, J. 27	Lang, L. 15	McCosham, H. 34
Kaufman, W. H. 17	Lang, V. 36	McDonald, J. A. 34
Kchnowicz 43	Lara, L. 10	McDowell, Miss M. 45
Keenan, L. H. 6	Larson, E. R. 41	McEvoy, P. 34
Kellar, H. A. 47	Larson, Miss E. 45	McKenzie, W. D. 35
Kelliher, D. 36	Lassi, R. 35	McKinmon, C. H. 34
Kelly, J. 36	Latchem, E. W. 35	McLaughlin, P. 35
Kennan, I. 44	Laub, E. F. C. 43	McMillan, A. H. 20
Kennedy, F. 38	Laukki, L. 34	McMurphy, J. J. 36
Kennedy, J. 35	Laur, L. 12	McNabb, J. W. 9
Kerl, T. 18	Law, J. 34	McNally, Ed. 23
Kerr, S. 27	Lawson, A. M. 31	McPherson, C. E. 43
Kimmons, I. 45	League of Humanity 37	McQuillen, P. 35
King, J. D. 35	Lee, H. 43	McWhirt, C. 34
Kingdom News, The 9	Lee, L. A. 8	MacDonald, E. E. 36
Kirchner, H. E. 14	Lefkowitz, H. 14	Machner, M. 18
Klabo, H. 32	Lefkowitz, N. 14	Mackenzie, R. 28
Klein, J. C. 18	LeGendre, L. N. 17, 48	Mackley, H. G. 14, 47
Kleinsouser, P. 43	Legoth, M. 33	Madelia News 13
	Leighton, F. W. 42	Mader, S. 16, 47

Mahoney, D. 15, 47	Miller, J. A. 16, 47	Normi, N. 37
Magon, R. 20	Miller, J. C. 10	Norocki, W.
Magruder, H. S. 42	Miller, P. 43	Oates, J. A. 34
Maher, W. E. 41	Miller, W. L. 35	Oberden, S. 6
Maihak, P. 35	Mills, J. 39	Oberlee, F. 6
Maken, A. E. 30	Mills, W. T. 24	Oberstadt, C. 29
Maki, L. 34	Mindinger, F. 30	O'Brien, J. L. 36
Maki, S. 42	Moes, J. 47	Oburn, E. 5
Manahan, J. 13	Mohr, C. E. 41	O'Connell, C. M. 48
Mansolf, H. 32	Monahan, P. 35	O'Connell, G. 35
Manus, J. D. 20	Monal, F. 7	O'Connell, D. 27
Marcowitz, L. B. 41	Monparler, F. 17	O'Day, T. 35
Marshall, S. 43	Monsky, H. 43	Oelco, I. 43
Martin, A. 36	Montgomery, E. L. 36	O'Hare, Mrs. K. R. 19, 37
Martin, F. A. 14	Montgomery, T. A. 23	O'Hair, V. V. 34
Martin, H. D. 41	Moore, A. 14	Ohlsen, C. 17
Martin, J. 36	Moore, H. 43	O'Leary, J. 22
Martin, J. 34	Moore, L. 36	Olivereau, L. 14
Martin, M. L. 44	Moran 43	Olsen, C. 35
Martin, P. 36	Moran, F. 35	Olsen, E. L. 35
Martin, W. 23	Moran, Wm. 34	Olson, O. 28
Martinez, T. 16	Morgan, F. 36	Olson, T. 18
Masson, F. 32	Morgan, J. E. 8	Oschner, O. 23
Masten, J. C. 17	Morgan, T. 42	Ostrom, E. 41
Mathewski, J. 30	Moser, F. 41	Oswald, J. W. 10
Mathson, M. 35	Mueller, H. 7	Otis, E. 25
Mattel, G. 10	Mufson, T. 44	Pahjola, A. 36
Matthey, Dr. W. C. 20	Muhlke, F. J. 41	Paine, E. 11
Mauer 43	Mullen, P. 14	Paine, M. 11
Maynard, G. 7	Mullis, F. 42	Pajol, J. 35
Mead, W. E. 16	Mulrooney, J. H. 35	Pancner, J. 34
Meents, J. 13	Murch, J. A. 43	Parenti, L. 34
Meier, E. 47	Murphy, H. 35	Parson, J. 35
Meirowitz, I. 27	Murphy, J. 35	Pasewalk, W. 35
Meitzen, C. 25	Murray, B. 35	Pass, J. 27
Melanos, S. 8	Munley, N. 23	Pass, M. 27
Melms, E. T. 24	Murphy, J. 36	Patton, F. 35
Milash, M. 24	Murphy, T. 33	Paul, D. 36
Menke, C. P. 48	Myers, H. B. 12	Penick, F. 41
Meredith, P. W. 18	Myles, N. 39	People's Church 39
Miama, C. 36	Nafe, G. 44	People's Council 37, 40
Merriman, W. 11	Nagler, L. B. 20	Pergande, O. 24
Metz, C. T. 8	Nearing, S. 26, 28, 37	Perruchon, P. 16
Metzdorf, Wm. 23	Nef, W. T. 34	Perry 14
Metzen, J. L. 6	Neilson, J. 35	Perry, G. H. 34
Metzler, R. 43	Neilson, V. J. 39	Persingerand, Prof.
Meyer, H. 11	Nelson, C. M. 48	E. E. 45
Meyers, D. M. 23	Nelson, F. 34	Peter, C. H. 11
Meyers, F. 27	Nelson, W. N. 36	Peterson, C. 10
Meyers, Mrs. F. 27	Nemser, H. 27	Peterson, J. 24
Meyers, J. C. 43	Netreba, C. 10	Petroshki, T. 42
Meyers, J. 48	Neuenschwander, A. 43	Petters, J. 15
Meyers, W. 29	N. Y. Bureau of	Pettigrew, R. F. 7, 22
Michaelvich, S. 33	Legal Advice 40	Phelan, J. B. 14
Michel, G. 23	Nikition, S. 33	Phelps-Dodge Corp. 11
Miller, A. A. 30	Non Partisan	Phillips, A. 9
Miller, F. 34	League 12, 13	Phillips, J. 34

Pierce, C. 21	Robinson, F. A. 42	Schoberg, C. B. 17, 27
Piggott Printing Co. 12	Robison, F. H. 20	Schubert, W. H. 14
Pignol, G. 44	Rockey, W. H. 47	Schultz, C. 9
Pilz, J. T. 39	Rodolph, C. C. 43	Schultz, H. M. 23
Pitkin, G. 34	Rogalski 10	Schultze, D. 10
Platin, E. R. 43	Rogers, B. 29	Schunke, C. S. 48
Poe, R. 35	Rogers, J. 24	Schurer, H. 25
Poenisch, G. 9	Rogers, M. 26	Schwaer, E. 15
Polaris, J. 10	Romero, F. M. 22, 47	Schwartz, J. 22
Pollok, T. 35	Rase, J. W. 42	Schwopke, R. 7
Poplovitch 43	Ross, J. 10, 34	Scott, R. 35
Potthast, J. 35	Ross, T. 35	Scott, T. 38
Povik, F. 30	Roth, A. 17, 48	Seaford, J. 29
Powell, R. 41	Rothfisher, C. 34	Seattle Call 12
Powell, W. 17	Rowan, J. 34	Seebach, J. C. 17
Plahn, C. 34	Rozansky, H. 22	Seidenberg, R. 43
Prager, R. P. 7	Rubenstein, H. J. 25	Selby, M. 7
Prashner, A. B. 34	Rubio, L. 23	Selzer, J. 14
Preith, B. 20	Ruby, J. 35	Senkis, T. 10
Price, J. 35	Ruck, J. 31	Shaffer, F. 22
Prince, A. G. 41	Rudolfky, A. 32	Shannon, E. 36
Prisse, W. 7	Russian Socialist 37	Shannon, J. 35
Proctor, W. D. 43	Ruthenberg, C. E. 26	Shea, J. 36
Prosser's, Rev. W. A. 40	Rutherford, J. F. 20	Shellenberger, J. G. 22
Quigley, E. 35	Ryan, J. F. 35	Sheridan, D. 34
Quinn, J. H. 42	Ryland, Rev. L. P. 44	Shioler, A. 17
Quinn, M. 35	Rynders, J. W. 11	Shintz, J. H. 31
Quinlan, J. 35	Saal, F. J. 17	Shiplacoff, A. I. 24
Rabitz, S. 30	Sadler, S. 27	Shuben, A. 43
Rabus, J. W. 32	Sahrbacher, C. 47	Shuren, S. 35
Ramp, F. 20	Saffores, B. 35	Shutt, Rev. E. C. 23
Randall, N. S. 12, 31	Salmon, B. J. 43	Sihto 35
Randolph, J. R. 18	Salty, G. 41	Siedneki, A. 30
Rantio, E. 37	Salv, T. 36	Sigwalt, G. 47
Rasmussen, P. 42	Sandberg, A. 16	Silver, E. 43
Ratti, J. J. 35	Sandberg, Wm. 43	Simons, A. 41
Rawe, H. 23	Sandin, M. 42	Sims, W. T. 5
Ray, W. 36	Sapper, M. 35	Sinclair, A. 34
Recker, R. 35	Sauer, C. 33	Singer, H. 30
Reed, J. 24, 26	Saylor, S. 48	Siro, V. 41
Reed, T. 41	Scarlett, S. 34	Sixtus, W. L. 29
Regan, R. 36	Schader, G. 32	Slaugh, P. 29
Regas Bros. 7	Schaefer, P. 20	Slovek, James 34
Reik, J. 30	Schafer, F. 47	Sinabel, P. 11
Reilly, F. 35	Schaper, W. A. 46	Smidt, G. H. 23
Reitz, E. S. 15	Scharf, O. 9	Smith, A. D. 32
Rem, G. R. 11	Schell, R. 28	Smith, A. 42
Rempfer, W. C. 6	Schellbach, P. 32	Smith, C. L. 35
Rey, M. 34	Schenck, C. T. 21	Smith, G. 14
Rheimer, H. 8	Schewing, A. 14	Smith, J. 35
Rice, C. H. 34	Schmalhausen, S. 44	Smith, L. 42
Richter, A. C. 7	Schneer, A. H. 44	Smith, M. J. 35
Rittenhouse, J. W. 38	Schnell, C. 35	Smith, T. 8
Rivera, L. 20	Schilter, C. 17	Smith, W. 34
Roberts, G. 34	Schimmel, E. A. 6	Social Labor Party 39
Robinette, E. 41	Schmidt, J. 42	Socialist Party 40
Robinson, C. 42	Schneider, H. 30, 42	Soper, A. E. 34

Name	Page	Name	Page	Name	Page
Sorenson, L.	42	Thomas, M. R.	41	Werner, L.	20
Somejkal, F.	11	Thompson, F. E.	21	Wernicke, A. H.	24
Spealman, F.	35	Thompson, J. P.	34	Werth, Rev. W. A.	20
Speed, G.	34	Tharaldson, T.	12	Westbrook, O. F.	6
Sprague, M.	35	Thulpape, G.	28	Westerland, F.	34
Spivak, J.	40	Tolishus, J. A.	17	Westphal, J.	35, 36
Stafford, Mrs. H.	8	Tori, L.	35	Wetter, P. C.	34
Stainaker, A. J.	21	Townley, A. C.	29	Wheeler, C. E.	42
Stanley, S.	42	Treseler, W. H.	42	Wheeler, O. O.	42
Stark, L.	35	Tucker, I. St. J.	20	Whitehead, A.	35
Stark, W. A.	6	Tummerscheit, G.	10	Wittrock, G.	41
Steadman, F.	18	Turner, J.	15	Weyh, W.	34
Steidel, H.	18, 33	Turner, J. I.	34	Whipple, Prof. L.	44
Steimer, M.	22	Tyrrel, J. W.	9	Whitaker, E.	41
Steinbeck, A. H.	19	Ungar, N.	42	Whitaker, R.	28
Steiner	43	United Verde Copper Co.	11	White, E.	6
Steinhauser, A.	23			White, J.	42
Stenberg, S.	34	Uren, F.	43	Whitehead, A. E.	37
Stenz, M.	33	Varrelman, F. A.	46	Wiegand, H.	45
Steinmolz, H.	9	Villareal, J.	10	Wiertola, W.	35
Stemler, Mrs. C. C.	16	Voetter, G. F.	35	Wiess, A.	18
Stenzel, B.	15	Vogel, P.	20	Wilhide, J. M.	24
Stepanovitch, F.	42	Vouderau, M.	10	W. I. I. U. Hall	40
Stephens, F.	25	Wagenknecht, A.	26	Wilson, A.	42
Sterenstein, S.	42	Wagner, C. H.	23	Wilson, R.	36
Stilson, J. V.	20	Wagner, D.	42	Williams, J.	15
St. John, V.	34	Wagner, W.	23	Williams, S.	35
Stock, H.	30	Wagoner, C.	9	Wingert,	43
Stokes, Mrs. R. P.	19	Waldron, Rev. C. H.	22, 48	Wipf, J.	43
Stopa, A. C.	17			Wishek, J. H.	23
Story, S.	23	Waldrop, W.	12	Winski, G.	35
Strand, F.	15	Wallace, D. H.	18	Witter, H.	24
Strangland	43	Wallberg, J.	35	Wold, C. A.	29
Stratemeyer, E. H.	5	Walsh, J.	34	Wolf, J. H.	15
Stredwick, H.	35	Walter, J. M.	42	Wolski, W.	35
Strode, G. V.	16	Walukus, B.	9	Wood, R. R.	42
Strom, G.	36	Wangerin, O.	42	Woodward, T.	28
Strul, P.	27	Ward, J. H.	26	Woodworth, C. H.	20
Sturm, L. H.	47	Ward, J.	35	Woelfle, J.	35
Schell, C. de	47	Ward, W. T.	36	Wortzmann, G.	42
Sugarman, A. L.	19	Warning, J. H.	34	Wortzmann, J.	42
Susoff, I.	43	Waters	43	Wright, W.	13
Swanson, O.	35	Watson, C.	9	Wurz, G. M.	42
Swift, G.	29	Weaver	32	Wusterbarth's F.	45
Swinbourne, W. J.	34	Webster, F. A.	44	Yanyar, A. L.	41
Sykes, J.	8	Wehmeyer, W. F.	18	Yarlott, G. R.	35
Tabib, C.	35	Weiershauser, G.	42	Yanyar, E.	22
Taichin, A. O.	31	Weiner, Miss Rose	29	Yarkiness, T.	32
Taliaferro, E. P.	7	Weinsberg, Dr. C. H.	25	Young, A.	26
Tanner, W. B.	25				
Tanner, Wm.	34	Weir, R.	35	Young, F.	29
Tantelli, V.	35	Weiss, G. C.	26	Young, I.	36
Taubert, G. H.	16, 47	Wells, E. P.	41	Youngman, P.	25
Tekah, Mrs. Mary	30	Wells, H. M.	27	Zang, H.	9
Tenegkeit, F.	6	Wenger, G.	35	Zerbe, W.	11
Teter, F.	21	Wenger, R. S.	42	Zimmerman, J.	25
Thomas, E.	24	Werner, A.	25	Zucker, M.	20

www.ingramcontent.com/pod-product-compliance
Lightning Source LLC
LaVergne TN
LVHW041459070426
835507LV00009B/691